5-Minute Mindfulness

SIMPLE DAILY SHORTCUTS TO
Transform Your Life

David B. Dillard-Wright, PhD, Heidi E. Spear, and Paula Munier

Adamsmedia

Avon, Massachusetts

For Father George, my godmother Susie, and my yogini Emma.

Published by
Adams Media, a division of F+W Media, Inc.
57 Littlefield Street, Avon, MA 02322. U.S.A.
www.adamsmedia.com

ISBN 10: 1-4405-2979-5
ISBN 13: 978-1-4405-2979-5
eISBN 10: 1-4405-3264-8
eISBN 13: 978-1-4405-3264-1

Printed in the United States of America.

10   9   8   7   6   5   4   3   2   1

Library of Congress Cataloging-in-Publication Data
is available from the publisher.

Contains material adapted and abridged from *Best You Ever*, by Rebecca Swanner, Eve Adamson, Carolyn Dean, MD, Rachel Laferriere, MS, RD, and Meera Lester, copyright © 2011 by F+W Media, Inc., ISBN 10: 1-4405-0657-4, ISBN 13: 978-1-4405-0657-4; *The Everything® Guide to Chakra Healing*, by Heidi E. Spear, copyright © 2011 by F+W Media, Inc., ISBN 10: 1-4405-2584-6, ISBN 13: 978-1-4405-2584-1; *The Everything® Guide to Meditation for Healthy Living*, by David B. Dillard-Wright, PhD, and Ravinder Jerath, MD, copyright © 2011 by F+W Media, Inc., ISBN 10: 1-4405-1088-1, ISBN 13: 978-1-4405-1088-5; *The Everything® Guide to Stress Management*, by Melissa Roberts, copyright © 2011 by F+W Media, Inc., ISBN 10: 1-4405-1087-3, ISBN 13: 978-1-4405-1087-8; *The Everything® Yoga Book*, by Cynthia Worby, MSW, MPH, RYT, copyright © 2002 by F+W Media, Inc., ISBN 10: 1-5806-2594-0, ISBN 13: 978-1-5806-2594-4; *Train Your Brain to Get Happy*, by Teresa Aubele, PhD, Stan Wenck, EdD, and Susan Reynolds, copyright © 2011 by F+W Media, Inc., ISBN 10: 1-4405-1181-0, ISBN 13: 978-1-4405-1181-3.

Many of the designations used by manufacturers and sellers to distinguish their product are claimed as trademarks. Where those designations appear in this book and Adams Media was aware of a trademark claim, the designations have been printed with initial capital letters.

Interior photographs © Ron Rinaldi, Digital Photography. Lotus illustration © Jupiterimages Corporation.

The information in this book should not be used for diagnosing or treating any health problem. Not all diet and exercise plans suit everyone. You should always consult a trained medical professional before starting a diet, taking any form of medication, or embarking on any fitness or weight-training program. The author and publisher disclaim any liability arising directly or indirectly from the use of this book.

This book is available at quantity discounts for bulk purchases.
For information, please call 1-800-289-0963.

CONTENTS

INTRODUCTION
WHAT IS MINDFULNESS?

"Yesterday is history. Tomorrow is a mystery. And today? Today is a gift. That's why we call it the present."

—BABATUNDE OLATUNJI

Live in the present.

Be here now.

Just breathe.

Great advice, but what does it really mean? And, how do you do it? You don't live on a mountaintop, or in a cave, or even in a monastery where you can devote endless hours to gazing at your navel in pursuit of enlightenment. You live in the so-called real world, where just getting through another 24/7 day is a challenge worthy of the Buddha.

But it doesn't have to be that way. You can master the art of mindfulness—and live in the present, be here now, and just breathe. You can learn to quiet your mind, listen to your body, and reconnect with your true self—deepening your experience of your own life.

And, you can do it anywhere, anytime. Mindfulness is a portable skill; once learned, you can carry with you and call on it whenever you need it—day by day, hour by hour, moment by moment.

In this book, we'll show you how to cultivate mindfulness in your everyday life in only minutes a day. You'll be amazed at how being more mindful can make a difference in the way you feel—body, mind, and soul. What's more, you'll discover the keys that open the door to your potential as a human being. You'll enter a vast and beautiful dimension of universal wisdom, wisdom you can call on to meet challenges, cope with difficulties, and resolve problems. You'll also learn to engage with your own life in ways that teach, heal, and enhance everything and everyone around you. It may take some work, but it is a labor of love you deserve to give yourself.

What Is Mindfulness?

Simply put, mindfulness is paying attention to your life *as you live it*. Learning to pay attention to your life as you live it can sometimes be challenging. You get caught up in your conflicting emotions, you drag yourself down with baggage from the past, you worry yourself with your unhappy visions of the future. Distracted by this barrage of thoughts and feelings and memories and imaginings, you forget to notice what's happening *now*, right in front of you.

CHAPTER 1

LIVING A MINDFUL LIFE

"You can become blind by seeing each day as a similar one. Each day is a different one, each day brings a miracle of its own. It's just a matter of paying attention to this miracle."

— PAULO COELHO

Odds are you've been practicing mindfulness all along without even knowing it. Most of us have experienced little aha! moments when we're doing something else entirely—while going for a jog, or driving to work, or even washing the dishes. Self-awareness often surprises us when we perform such simple, methodical tasks that free the mind from the seemingly endless loops of thoughts and feelings that can distract us from the moment at hand. The sort of activities that can induce such unexpected mindfulness run the gamut of human experience, including:

- **Sports.** Athletes frequently speak of being "in the zone"—the mental freedom they experience when the body is completely involved in meeting a challenge, such as running a long distance or climbing a steep incline.
- **Mothering.** Mothers know the serenity that sets in as they sing a child to sleep or rock a baby in their arms. This maternal peace can begin with breastfeeding, which not only enhances the bonding process with the infant but also deepens the perception of the life force itself.
- **Strenuous work.** The focus required to perform vigorous physical labor, such as carrying heavy loads with great care or chopping wood, can bring uncommon mind–body awareness.

- **Knitting.** The rhythm of the clacking needles, the feel of the soft yarn between your fingers, the persistent lull of the contiguous stitches—that's the mindmeld of knitting that lets enlightenment happen.
- **Gardening.** Digging in the dirt not only evokes the sense of child's play we experienced as kids in the sandbox, it also puts us back in touch—literally—with Mother Earth. Both playing and communing with nature require living in the moment and are therefore mindful activities.
- **Chores.** Familiar tasks—those so familiar that you can do them "in your sleep"—often create space for the mind to relax and drop into the present moment.

In these instances, it is the realization—without thought or feeling—that you are participating in the moment that brings you into the state of mindfulness. Learn to cultivate this state more often and for longer periods of time, and you are on your way to enlightenment.

MINDFUL YOU, HEALTHY YOU

If discovering greater meaning and purpose in life wasn't reason enough to convince us, the physical benefits of mindfulness should be. Over the past few decades, mounting scientific evidence confirms that mindfulness can reduce the harmful effects of our stressful lifestyles, making us healthier, as well as happier.

Want to have more energy?
Reduce the risk of a heart attack?
Control depression and anxiety?

Science now shows us that we don't always have to reach for a pill bottle. There are alternative means of enhancing our well-being—and mindfulness is prime among them. Through various mindfulness techniques—many centuries if not millennia old—we can relearn the time-honored lessons lost in our fast-paced, technology-driven societies. At the same time, technology and science can help us to better understand these ancient practices, revealing how and why they actually work.

Throughout the ages, every society has created its unique set of mindfulness techniques. Many of these techniques have morphed over time, adapting to changing morés and customs. Some traditions have influenced one another in profound ways, such as yoga and Buddhism. Today, we see that same confluence happening even in secular settings. For instance, many stress-reduction programs incorporate yoga postures and Buddhist meditation techniques.

In this book, you will find a mixture of the old and the new, the scientific and the philosophic, the anecdotal and the empirical—all of which support the fact that mindfulness really does promote healthy living.

The Mindfulness Toolbox

Thanks to this wealth of knowledge and tradition, we can transform ourselves into creatures of mindfulness rather than creatures of habit. Some of the most effective old and new mindfulness tools include:

- Meditation
- Prayer
- Yoga
- Tai Chi
- Deep breathing
- Visualization
- Massage

- Reiki
- Aromatherapy
- Music therapy
- Exercise
- Hypnosis
- Biofeedback

THE MANY FACES OF MINDFULNESS

There are many approaches to mindfulness. Some may appear simple, practical, and easy to understand; others may seem otherworldly, impractical, and esoteric. Some styles may have proven too religious to appeal to you or not spiritual enough.

In *5-Minute Mindfulness*, you'll learn how to choose—and use—the best tools for your own body, mind, and soul. To find the mindfulness approach that best addresses your individual needs, we'll look at what each offers and decide which features are suitable—for you. It's not necessary to limit yourself to one technique. By incorporating what reflects your unique nature, whether it is two or three styles or a dozen, you will be able to design a mindfulness practice that reflects all that you are and that encourages you to be all you can be.

There are as many ways to practice mindfulness as there are personality types. You'll want to use the tools that best suit your personality. Exploring the many dimensions of mindfulness can be satisfying in itself, but taking your attitudes and habits into account can help you discover the best approach for you.

THE MINDFULNESS STYLE QUIZ

1. When you're stressed out, you like to wind down by:
- A. Hanging out with friends
- B. Watching the Discovery Channel on TV
- C. Working out
- D. Getting a massage

2. You feel closest to God when you:
- A. Go on retreat
- B. You don't believe in God
- C. Attend services at your favorite place of worship
- D. Take a walk in the woods

3. When a conflict arises with a colleague at work, you:
- A. Go above his/her head
- B. Negotiate a solution

C. Confront him/her

D. Disappear into your office

4. **You're late for an important appointment, and you're stuck in traffic. You:**

    A. Text whomever you are meeting every five minutes with an update

    B. Recalculate the time it will take you to get there every five minutes

    C. Use this unexpected downtime to make a few calls

    D. Turn the music on louder and rock out

5. **It's past bedtime, and the kids are tired and cranky and so are you. You:**

    A. Tuck them in and tell them a bedtime story

    B. Negotiate a bedtime truce with milk and cookies

    C. Yell at them to go to bed

    D. Run them a warm bath and pour yourself a glass of wine

6. **Your tax accountant made a mistake, and you find out you owe the IRS thousands of dollars you don't have. You:**

    A. Change accountants

    B. Negotiate a settlement with the IRS yourself

    C. Threaten to sue your accountant unless he/she negotiates a settlement on your behalf

    D. Worry yourself half to death before doing anything about it

7. **When you're alone, you like to:**

    A. Write, paint, play music

    B. Read a good book

    C. Exercise

    D. Dance naked around the house

8. **For you, being with people:**

    A. Sometimes energizes you; sometimes tires you

    B. Energizes you

C. Almost always tires you

D. Is not your first choice; you prefer to be alone

9. For you, being alone is:

A. An opportunity to create

B. An opportunity to reflect

C. Boring

D. Heaven

10. Most nights you eat:

A. Whatever you can cobble together

B. Take-out in front of the TV

C. Dinner with family and/or friends

D. Clean food

11. When you are upset, you:

A. Know you'll figure it out eventually

B. Mull it over on your own

C. Talk it over with your best friend

D. Do something fun to help you forget about it

12. When people close to you are upset, you:

A. Insist they tell you all about it right away

B. Leave them alone until they want to talk about it

C. Try to cheer them up

D. Avoid them until they get over it

13. The quality you most admire in yourself is:

A. Intuition

B. Intelligence

C. Productivity

D. Imagination

If you checked mostly As, then you are:

THE SEER

You are intuitive when evaluating something new, first visualizing your involvement before making any decisions. Impressions and dreams are meaningful in the process, and you often pay attention to your hunches. The Seer has strong auditory senses and does well with chant, prayer, and sound support in a mindfulness practice. Seers make rapid progress in the early stages of meditation but falter once the visual images become stale. To receive maximum health benefit from meditation, Seers should stretch their capacities by meditating on silence and the ineffable.

If you checked mostly Bs, then you are:

THE THINKER

You are analytical when presented with new information; an idea has to make sense before you agree to it. You employ a methodical approach when learning a skill and prefer to go by a checklist when performing tasks. The Thinker has a well-developed tactile sense, depending on the sense of touch to balance analytical processes. This ability works well with a mindfulness practice that employs physical conditioning and sequential development of the body's powers. The self-discipline required for slow, deep breathing—which yields immediate physiological responses in meditation—will come easily to Thinkers, but they will have a harder time cultivating feelings of universal goodwill necessary to bring meditation to full fruition.

If you checked mostly Cs, then you are:

THE EXECUTOR

You don't like to waste time or energy with nonessentials; getting the job done is what satisfies you the most. Teamwork and feedback are important, and you are not derailed by interferences or delays. The Executor is visually oriented and does well with systems that use images, icons, and symbols. To receive maximum stress reduction from meditation, Executors will need to learn to tolerate ambiguity and open-endedness. On the plus side, Executors have a strong ability to stay on task, which makes establishing a practice relatively easy.

If you checked mostly Ds, then you are:

THE FEELER

You enjoy being insulated from the outside world and treasure your own time and space. You will consider new activities if they don't require great adjustments to your lifestyle, and you will seek a few opinions before going ahead. The Feeler has cultivated a gustatory approach to living, appreciating the sensate side of life. A system that includes full-sense involvement, such as ritual meditation, will satisfy this type. The propensity for solitude will make Feelers natural meditators, but, for maximum well-being, Feelers should coax themselves toward spiritual community to sustain themselves over the long haul.

Note: This is just a general guide. Many of us are a combination of these types, and you may relate to some qualities from every type. To get the most from your practice, you should be prepared to explore whatever mindfulness tools and techniques resonate with you regardless of type.

GOOD TO THE CORE

Mindfulness at the core of life infuses every act with meaning and richness. It doesn't have to be a separate "special" event that takes us away from our responsibilities or leisure. Rather, it's an ongoing process that is part of everything we do and everything we are. You'll get as much from your mindfulness practice as you give it, more so if you articulate your intentions. Here are some intentions that might resonate with you:

FREEDOM FROM STRESS

Life is full of stressful conditions, whether you are at work, on vacation, or just doing nothing. Mindfulness can increase your awareness of when and where you're feeling stress. Once you are mindful of what triggers your stress response, you can use mindfulness practices (such as yoga and meditation) to minimize its effect on you.

A POSITIVE ATTITUDE

Mindfulness doesn't mean you will avoid powerful emotions — positive or negative. When you cultivate mindfulness, you learn to observe your life and your emotions without attaching negative or positive judgments to them. You begin to see yourself and your life just as it is as it unfolds. From that place of nonjudgmental awareness, you develop a positive attitude because what's happening in your life isn't good or bad: It just *is*. And, there's beauty to be found in the present moment.

SUCCESS AT WHAT YOU DO

Whether you are an artist, parent, spouse, or technician, there is always room for improvement. Mindfulness can help you focus your attention on what you are doing and hone your skills to higher levels. And, just as mindfulness is a continuing process, so is "becoming better."

ENLIGHTENMENT

Who doesn't want to attain enlightenment? As you go through life, your light becomes brighter when the inner life is developed in unison with the outer life. This is the subtle balance that mindfulness helps us maintain.

As we prepare to explore this process and to experience the positive effects of mindfulness on mind, body, and spirit, let's begin by setting an intention for the journey on which we are about to embark.

Mindfulness Now: Set Your Intention

Think of the one aspect of your life that would most benefit from a more mindful approach.

For example, do you wish you had more patience when dealing with your kids?

Would your health improve if you were more aware of your physical body and took better care of it? Is your job such a source of stress you'd be better off finding a new one?

Whatever your intention, hold it in your mind for a moment. Close your eyes, and breathe deeply. Inhale, and breathe in what you need in your life. Exhale, and breathe out what no longer serves you.

For example:
Breathe in love; exhale loneliness.
Breathe in courage; exhale fear.
Breathe in patience; exhale irritability.
Continue for several more rounds of breath. After five minutes, repeat your intention, and open your eyes.
We are ready to begin.

"The secret of health for both mind and body is not to mourn for the past, worry about the future, or anticipate troubles, but to live in the present moment wisely and earnestly."

— BUDDHA

CHAPTER 2
STRESS RELIEF FOR YOUR BRAIN

"The mind is like a crazy monkey, which leaps about and never stays in one place."

—CHÖGYAM TRUNGPA RINPOCHE

It's 2:00 A.M. and you can't sleep. Your mind keeps turning over and over:

I should never have said that to my mother.
My boss is going to kill me if I don't finish that report by Friday.
I really need to change the oil in my car.
My love life is a joke.
I wonder if I should get that mole on my shoulder checked out.
We're going to starve if I don't pick up some groceries soon.
If I could just fall asleep within the next ten minutes, I'd get 4½ hours of sleep.

On and on it goes, that endless chatter in your head that you can never really switch off long enough to get a decent night's sleep, much less stop and smell the roses. The Buddhists call it "monkey mind." Taming the monkey mind means taming the stress in your life. It means cultivating mindfulness.

HOW STRESSED OUT IS TOO STRESSED OUT?
All of us have experienced some kind of stress, and many of us experience chronic stress every day of our lives. Some of us handle stress pretty well, even when it is extreme. Others are far less able to handle

11

stress. What's the difference? Some of it may be genetic; many research-ers believe that people have an inherited level of stress tolerance. Some people can take a lot and still feel great and, in fact, do their best work under stress. Other people require very low-stress lives to productively function. But, whether you're blessed with good stress genes or not so good, you can learn to reduce your stress level. And, it's critical to your well-being that you do.

> *"Stress is basically a disconnection from the earth, a forgetting of the breath. Stress is an ignorant state. It believes that everything is an emergency. Nothing is that important. Just lie down."*
>
> —NATALIE GOLDBERG

Stress is a function of our human survival instinct. Our bodies are pro-grammed to shift into high gear whenever we are faced with danger. If you should suddenly find yourself in a dangerous situation—you step in front of a speeding car, you lose your balance and teeter on the edge of a cliff, you call your boss a moron when he is standing right behind you—your body will react to this stress in a way designed to ensure your survival.

Here's what happens:

1. **Your cerebral cortex sends an alarm message to your hypothala-mus, the part of your brain that releases the chemicals that create the stress response. Anything your brain** *perceives* **as stress will cause this effect, whether or not you are in any real danger.**
2. **Your hypothalamus releases chemicals that stimulate your sympa-thetic nervous system to prepare for danger.**
3. **Your nervous system reacts by raising your heart rate, respiration rate, and blood pressure. Everything gets "turned up."**

4. **Your muscles tense, preparing for action.** Blood moves away from the extremities and your digestive system into your muscles and brain. Blood sugars are mobilized to travel where they will be needed most.
5. **Your senses get sharper.** You can hear better, see better, smell better, taste better. Even your sense of touch becomes more sensitive.

Physiologist Walter B. Cannon coined the phrase "fight or flight" to describe these biochemical changes, which literally prepare you for the effort required to either confront or run from whatever is threatening you. Every time you feel stressed, the stress hormones adrenaline and cortisol flood your bloodstream, giving you the boost of strength and energy you need to either subdue that lion if you think you can or run like the dickens.

Adrenaline increases your heart rate and your breathing rate and sends blood straight to your vital organs so they can work better, and cortisol flows through your body to keep the stress response going as long as the stress continues.

Techno Stress

Not many of us face down lions every day, but our modern life moves so quickly that keeping up is inherently stressful. Technology may allow us to do ten times more in a fraction of the time, but the stress associated with our multitasking, 24/7 lifestyle can negate whatever gains technology may bring us.

It's a rush that can prove addictive. But, if you were to experience the constant release of adrenaline and cortisol every day, eventually that rush would grow tiresome, quite literally. Stress wipes us out, causing exhaustion, physical pain, a decrease in the ability to concentrate and remember, frustration, irritability, insomnia, and even violent episodes.

Too much stress does more than just overwhelm our system with too much adrenaline and cortisol; it interferes with the production of hormones that help us maintain balance and equanimity:

Serotonin is the hormone that helps you get a good night's sleep. Produced in the pineal gland, deep inside your brain, serotonin controls your body clock by converting into melatonin and then converting back into serotonin over the course of a twenty-four-hour day. This process regulates your energy, body temperature, and sleep cycle. The serotonin cycle synchronizes with the cycle of the sun, regulating itself according to exposure to daylight and darkness, which is why some people who are rarely exposed to the sun, such as those in northern climates, experience seasonal depression during the long, dark winter months—their serotonin production gets out of whack. Stress can throw it out of whack, too, and one result is the inability to sleep well. People under stress often experience a disturbed sleep cycle, manifesting itself as insomnia or an excessive need to sleep because the sleep isn't productive.

Noradrenaline is a hormone produced by your adrenal glands, cousin to the adrenaline that your body releases in times of stress to give you that extra chance at survival. Noradrenaline is related to your daily cycle of energy. Too much stress can disrupt your body's production of noradrenaline, leaving you with a profound lack of energy and motivation. It's that feeling you get when you just want to sit and stare at the television even though you have a long list of things you absolutely have to do. If your noradrenaline production is disrupted, you'll probably just keep sitting there, watching television. You simply won't have the energy to get anything done.

Dopamine is a hormone linked to the release of endorphins in your brain. Endorphins help kill pain. Chemically, they are related to opiate substances, such as morphine and heroin, and, if you are injured, your body releases endorphins to help you function. When stress compromises your body's ability to produce dopamine, it also compromises your body's ability to produce endorphins, so you become more sensitive to pain. Dopamine is responsible for that wonderful feeling you get from doing things you enjoy. It makes you feel happy about life itself. Too much stress, too little dopamine—and nothing seems fun or pleasurable anymore. You feel flat. You feel depressed.

MAXING OUT ON STRESS

We already know that stress causes your cerebral cortex to begin a process that results in the release of chemicals to prepare your body to handle danger. But, what else goes on in your brain when you are under too much stress? At first, you think more clearly and respond more quickly. But, after you've reached your stress tolerance point, your brain begins to malfunction. You forget things. You lose things. You can't concentrate. You lose your willpower and indulge in bad habits, such as drinking, smoking, or eating too much.

The production of the chemicals from the stress response that makes the brain react more quickly and think more sharply is directly related to the depletion of other chemicals that, under too much stress, keeps you from thinking effectively or reacting quickly. Eventually, any positive effects are overwhelmed by the negative. Remember the last time you took a particularly stressful exam? At first, odds are the answers to the test came to you without hesitation. However, three hours into the test and you could barely remember which end of the pencil to use to fill in those endless, little circles.

STRESS ON YOUR MIND

Lions aside, stressors affecting us in today's world are seemingly endless. Some of the most stressful include:

- Work pressure
- Impending important events
- Relationship problems with a spouse, child, or parent
- The death of a loved one

Any major life change can result in mental stress, depending on how the mind interprets the event, and even when an event is positive—a marriage, a graduation, a new job, a Caribbean cruise—the change it represents, even if temporary, can be overwhelming.

Mental stress can result in low self-esteem, a negative outlook on life, cynicism, or the desire for isolation as the mind attempts to justify and, in any way possible, stop the stress. (If you've ever had an extremely stressful week and want nothing more than to spend the entire weekend alone in bed with a good book and the remote control, you've experienced the mind attempting to regain its equilibrium.) Allow stress to continue for too long, and you could suffer burnout, panic attacks, severe depression, or even a nervous breakdown.

Take This Job

If your job stresses you out, you are not alone. According to the American Institute of Stress:

- One million people miss work every day due to stress-related complaints.
- Nearly half of all American workers suffer from symptoms of burnout or severe job-related stress that impairs or impedes functioning.
- Job stress costs U.S. industries $300 billion every year in absenteeism; diminished productivity; employee turnover; and direct medical, legal, and insurance fees. Between 60 and 80 percent of industrial accidents are attributed to stress.
- Once rare, workers' compensation awards for job stress have now become common.
- Nine out of ten job-stress suits are successful, with an average payout of more than four times the payout for injury claims.

Mental stress can be particularly dangerous because you can ignore it more easily than you can a physical illness. Yet, it is just as powerful and just as harmful to the body and to your life.

MINDFULNESS TO THE RESCUE

As we have seen, stress really is all in your mind—because that's where the stress response begins. Right or wrong, when your brain reads danger, the fight-or-flight response kicks in.

Become mindful, and you can short-circuit that stress response. You can learn to step back and see your thoughts and emotions like the weather—constantly changing but ultimately not very important. You can wean yourself off the roller coaster of the stress response and find a more level state of being, increasing your energy level and state of overall health. Initially, this may be disconcerting if you have lived with inner turmoil for years or decades. Having a peaceful state of mind may even feel irresponsible because you have come to think of out-of-control emotions as somehow productive.

Fear and anxiety don't solve problems. Unconsciously, you may be using powerful emotions as a substitute for constructive action. Mindfulness takes away the worries and, with them, your defenses and excuses. You can see problems and the resources needed to face those problems more clearly. While many exaggerated claims have been made about the potential of mindfulness to generate worldly success, it is true that a sensible program can help you achieve and maintain a more relaxed state of mind; over time, this can lead you to a greater quality of life, including greater productivity and quality of work.

SYMPATHETIC AND PARASYMPATHETIC BALANCE

To understand how mindfulness works, you should understand the connections between the sympathetic and parasympathetic nervous systems. When you sleep, your nervous system shifts back and forth between sympathetic-dominant and parasympathetic-dominant states about every 1½ hours. Rapid eye movement (REM) sleep, the state that induces vivid dreaming, is a sympathetic-dominant state. In this part of the sleep cycle, your mind remains very active, much as it is in your waking life. By contrast, the parasympathetic-dominant state is typically characterized by dreamless sleep; this is when the rejuvenation of brain and body takes place.

In deep sleep, the rhythm of breathing synchronizes with brain waves. Breathing slows and so do your brain waves. Without inducing actual sleep, meditation mimics what happens in dreamless sleep. Your blood pressure and pulse go down, stress hormones are inhibited, and conscious awareness goes into a more subdued state.

HARNESSING THE POWER OF MEDITATION

The mindfulness tool we use to settle our monkey mind is meditation. Meditation, combined with deep breathing, can reduce the everyday effects of stress—it can even prevent and treat chronic disorders. Physiological benefits include:

- Reduced heart rate, blood pressure, and cholesterol levels
- Lower stress levels
- Less anxiety and other emotional disorders
- Increased concentration and spatial memory
- Pain reduction

Mindfulness works by balancing the fight-or-flight response with parasympathetic activity, getting the body to go into a rest and recuperation mode. Meditation and deep breathing induce this resting state through two principal means: slowing the rate of breathing and generating nonjudgmental thought patterns.

MONKEY MIND–BODY LOOPS

When we're caught up in monkey mind, we often start chasing "loops" that eventually take over by chasing us. These loops rob us of our sense of well-being; they keep us going back and forth, round and round. Since the mind and body are connected, stress that starts in the mind affects the body. Following are some of the monkey mind–body loops you may be struggling with.

THE STRESS–LETHARGY LOOP

The continual demands of your responsibilities may have you racing to resolve every crisis. This stress is followed by periods of depletion that allow only enough time and energy to recuperate to meet the next demand. In time, you may feel that crises beset you at every turn—and you have no time for relaxing or doing the things you really want to do. You alternate between overwork and oversleep. If you're often wondering "What if?," you may be caught in the stress–lethargy loop.

THE ANXIETY–FEAR LOOP

You may have faced serious disruptions in your life, and they confirmed your worst fears. You expect those disruptions to rear their ugly heads again, and you're not sure you can handle them when that happens. You alternate between hesitation and restlessness. If you're often worried about the future, you may be stranded in the anxiety–fear loop.

THE PANIC–CONTROL LOOP

You've had everything in your life pretty well managed the way you wanted, but now little things seem to be slipping out of your control. The more this happens, the more you try to find ways to get things back on track—often by trying to control and/or micromanage the people around you. You alternate between feeling overwhelmed and feeling frustrated. If you're asking "Why me?" a lot, you may be in the panic–control loop.

THE ANGER–DEPRESSION LOOP

You've had to deal with some menacing people and situations, but you didn't do anything about it. Now you feel defeated; you simply cannot marshal the energy to act. You alternate between irritability and sluggishness. If you find yourself frequently saying "No way!," you may be in the anger–depression loop.

THE BITTERNESS–ISOLATION LOOP

You've made it through some difficult times in the past, and they've left their mark on you. So, you avoid people and places that remind you of the past, although you'd like to return to the way you used to be. You alternate between mistrust and lack of motivation. If you find yourself frequently referring to the past, you may be in the bitterness–isolation loop.

Wring Out Your Brain

All day, every day, you absorb information and impressions from the outside world like a sponge—not all of it beneficial. Meditation is one way to wring out the sponge, squeezing out whatever you don't want or need. It is preventive medicine for the spirit, a refreshing pause for the mind, and a reservoir of calm for the emotions.

GETTING OUT OF THE LOOP USING MEDITATION

How does meditation help you break out of the monkey mind–body loops? All of these loops have their basis in the sympathetic/parasympathetic balance. Meditation helps you cut the looping short by hitting the "reset" button. The restorative functions of the parasympathetic system counterbalance the active energies of the sympathetic nervous system. On an emotional level, the sense of well-being you feel counteracts the negative emotions that feed into the loop.

THE LOOP RX

Meditation allows you to stop running around the hamster wheel of the loops and regain your perspective. While you can benefit from all the various meditation techniques, certain approaches are more effective in fighting some loops than others. The following list will help you isolate the approach that will work best to quiet your monkey mind:

Transience—Easy Come, Easy Go: See the inevitable ebb and flow of all things. Problems—and their solutions—are transient: They come and go like the rising and falling tides. When you see this rhythm in life, you're less likely to fall into the stress–lethargy loop.

The Transience Exercise: Watch the clouds passing overhead, and imagine that each cloud is a problem in your life. Tag each one—unpaid bills, tight deadlines, piles of laundry, etc.—and watch it float across the sky and out of view. You can do this any time you find yourself stressing out over having too much to do or deal with—just close your eyes wherever you are, and imagine those clouds moving in and out of your mind.

Compassion—Love Really Is the Answer: Develop an appreciation for life in all its aspects. Going through life with such an appreciation encourages generosity and compassion. When you focus on loving-kindness toward yourself and others, anxiety and fear will no longer dominate your feelings.

The Compassion Exercise: Close your eyes; draw your attention inward to your heart center. Picture your tender heart, and say to yourself, *May I be brave and wise and happy.* Repeat this a few times in your mind. Next, think of someone you love whose courage and compassion you admire. Picture that person in your mind, and repeat this thought: *May you be brave and wise and happy.* Then picture someone you find challenging or difficult, and address this person in the same way: *May you be brave and wise and happy.* Finally, broaden your statement to include everyone: *May all beings be brave and wise and happy.* Try this whenever you feel overwhelmed by fear or anxiety.

Surrender—No More Control Freak: Let go of your belief that you must be in charge of everything and everyone. The more persistently you hang on to your control issues, the more other people will resist—and resent—you. By abandoning this approach, you also abandon the panic–control loop.

The Surrender Exercise: The next time you're about to panic over the imperfect state of your life, stop yourself before you start trying to fix anything—or anyone. Find a quiet corner away from the source of your panic—the messy kitchen, the uncooperative colleague, the unruly kids—and sit down. Make a list of the things you want to change: your roommate's untidiness, your colleague's bad work ethic, your kids' tantrums. Cross out whatever you cannot change. Hint: You can't change others; you can only change yourself. Now, close your eyes, and repeat the Serenity Prayer: *God grant me the serenity to accept the things I cannot change, the courage to change the things I can, and the wisdom to know the difference.*

Detachment—On a Clear Day You Can See Forever: Recognize that you are not attached to the conditions of your life. View whatever you have done—or have not done—with objectivity. Casting a clear eye on your situation helps you release any feelings of resentment or regret—freeing you to act in your best interest. This helps you overcome the anger–depression loop.

The Detachment Exercise: The next time you start beating yourself up about the choices you have made, remind yourself that you are not your choices:

I am not my choices. I am peace.
I am not my choices. I am love.
I am not my choices. I am clarity.

Repeat until you are clear on what course of action you should take. If you are still unable to decide what to do, simply toss a coin—heads or tails—and act accordingly. Do this for one day for every decision, large or small, and by the end of the day, you will see that your choices do not define you.

Unity with Life—Join the Party: Cultivate a rapport with those around you. No matter how different or unfamiliar the territory, discover the essential qualities you have in common with others. Discovering this unity can remedy the bitterness–isolation loop.

The Unity Exercise: Loneliness is often born of past disappointments. But isolating yourself from others to avoid getting hurt simply breeds more bitterness. You can break this cycle by acknowledging that we are all one, all connected, all part of the energy of the universe. The next time you are feeling isolated, go somewhere where you can be one among many—a city park, a place of worship, a library, a yoga class. Sit among your fellow human beings, and breathe in the energy of community. Feel this vibration, and call on this energy when you interact with everyone in your life.

The 5-Minute Antidote to Autopilot

The antidote to autopilot is mindfulness. In the middle of your busy day, stop and notice a tree outside the window, a picture on your desk, or that beautiful apple on your lunch tray. Take several minutes to just explore the object with one or more of your senses. You have just practiced awareness—and banished autopilot.

> *"We are what we think. All that we are arises with our thoughts. With our thoughts, we make the world."*

— BUDDHA

CHAPTER 3

GOODBYE, MONKEY MIND

"The affairs of the world will go on forever. Do not delay the practice of meditation."

—Milarepa

If you think you don't have the time, energy, or inclination to meditate, think again. Meditation is a wake-up call you don't want to miss—promising you not only greater well-being but also a stronger sense of self. It helps you navigate the labyrinth of your own self-knowledge as you explore various states and stages.

ENLIGHTENMENT

Enlightenment is the expressed goal of many meditation traditions, from Buddhism to yoga. But, it may also be the most elusive thing to achieve. The best way to see this goal is to recognize that we rarely use most of our emotional, intellectual, and physical potential in positive ways. It is as if these areas of our life run on high wattage the way a light bulb does, but the power to illuminate them is very low. When meditation increases the power, these functions "light up," and when all are working in sync, we are "enlightened."

IMPERMANENCE

In meditation, your outer, external reality is viewed as transitory and impermanent. You can uncover the true reality—that is, your permanent self—through meditation. Who you really are is not affected by your experience in the so-called real world, however bad or good. So,

24

when difficult or challenging things happen, you can remember that your permanent self remains unaffected—and let go of those experiences that might otherwise haunt you.

ATTENTION

Paying attention is the careful observation of your body, emotions, moods, thoughts, and real-time experiences. Paying attention includes observation of your thoughts themselves. For example, when you look at a picture of a hamburger and milkshake, you may be struck by hunger—or rather the *thought* of hunger. Trace that thought to its origin if possible. Ask yourself where it's coming from:

- A true sensation from your growling empty stomach (because you haven't eaten all day and really are hungry)
- A mental picture of a past event (the great burgers you had last week at that cookout)
- An emotional picture of feeling satiated (the happy memories you associate with milkshakes your grandmother made for you when you were a child)

NONATTACHMENT

Being nonattached does not mean cutting yourself off from yourself or other people. Instead, meditation allows us to detach from the preoccupations that bedevil our monkey minds, absorbing our attention, energy, and vitality long after we really need them. By practicing nonattachment in a constructive way, we can ensure that we address the issues that come up as they present themselves—and then release them.

TRANSFORMATION

Transformation is the morphing of one form of energy into another. We do this constantly while breathing, eating, and sleeping. Conscious transformation means noting the energy you use as you use it—helping you use your energy more effectively and move from one form to another more smoothly.

SET THE STAGE FOR MEDITATION

Establish a daily meditation practice, and you will build a foundation for leading a mindful life. That's why it's called practice: the more you do it, the more effective it is. And, the easier it is to re-create the peace you experience in meditation during the rest of your life. Think of meditation as your mind's oasis, a place where, monkey mind silenced, you can refresh yourself. Set up your oasis, get comfortable there, and you can retreat to it at will.

YOUR SACRED SPACE

In the beginning, you will want to select a place where you can begin your practice and continue at your pace, in your own style, without distraction. Ideally, this would be a dedicated room or garden. If you can't dedicate an entire room, choose a corner of a main room that you can partition with a screen or furniture. (Don't use a closet or bathroom because this subconsciously marginalizes your practice.) If your sacred space will be outside, make sure you have a comfortable chair, bench, or cushion, and avoid extremes of heat and cold.

Obviously, a place where interference is at a minimum is ideal. When you start to focus your attention inward, the list of potential distractions is endless—and sometimes unexpected:

Clutter. A cluttered space is a distraction. Just as your bedroom should be reserved for sleeping and making love if you are to invite rest and intimacy into your life, so should your meditation space be reserved for meditation if you are to invite serenity and mindfulness into your life. An orderly, clean environment encourages the feeling of readiness and ease.

Electronics. Turn off your cell phone—and no computers or tablets or radios or televisions. Your meditation space should be electronics-free.

Foot traffic. Most of all, your meditation space should not be a place where foot traffic will disrupt your focus. An area where others will be eating, ironing, or watching television isn't a good choice. Members of your household should not be passing through your space. This will be your sanctuary, so it should offer peace and privacy from the outside world.

Lighting. Even the low buzz of fluorescent lighting can prove an annoyance that detracts from your practice. Allow the natural environment to prevail. Natural light is best—the more windows, the better. With so many of us stuck in cubicles all day, we often miss the rhythms of nature. This cuts us off from positive influences and a connection with the natural world that can prove so helpful in enhancing mindfulness.

Music. Even music can be distracting—when it's the wrong music. Be careful when you choose music. Some sounds can stimulate thinking and memories; others can induce lethargy. You will also want a sound system that allows for continuous play or programmed selections so you don't have to keep adjusting it.

A Space with a View

A natural vista would be helpful for beginning a meditation practice. Trees, bodies of water, and patches of earth are visual aids for detaching from thoughts and emotions. Of course, not everyone has the advantage of living near scenic sites. You could create one of your own.

THE LESSONS OF DISTRACTION

Completely eliminating distractions is neither possible nor desirable; everything is grist for the mill of meditation—even, and especially, the annoying elements in our spaces! Behind every distraction is some attachment waiting to be uncovered and diffused, some adjustment in attitude that needs to be made. So strive to have a clean, orderly, inspiring, out-of-the-way place to meditate but realize that this will never entirely be the case. Even monks and nuns living the cloistered life have physical and mental distractions, just like the rest of us. Distractions sometimes can only be endured or transcended—not eliminated.

THE ACCOUTREMENTS OF MINDFULNESS

Your meditation oasis should reflect your personal tastes and your goals. You can experiment with this, choosing those elements that suit your personality and home décor. No matter which type of meditation you work with—traditional, secular, or your own eclectic version—you'll need some accessories in the beginning and throughout your meditation practice.

Comfort is an important concern. You may be spending some time in this space, and you don't want to become discouraged because it feels uncomfortable. You should be able to maintain a comfortable temperature, but keep a warm blanket or throw nearby in case it gets drafty.

The wall space that surrounds you is another consideration. You may want a blank canvas for your initial meditation practice, or you may feel more at ease with the usual décor. Then, again, you may want to choose special wall hangings, a set of favorite prints, a painting, or a Thangka (a Tibetan silk painting and textile object depicting scenes that encourage meditation and healing).

Whether you have access to a lot of natural light or depend on artificial sources, make sure the light can be adjusted. Candles are often used for focus in meditation, but they can pose safety problems if not supported securely. Likewise, incense should be burned in containers that will catch the ashes.

Plants and flowers are other additions to the meditation space that can lend a connection to nature and create a fresh atmosphere. You can even use plants as visual reminders of your meditation practice. Each time you water the plants, you will be reminded that you will also need the refreshment of a meditation session. And, as the plants grow, so will your proficiency in personal growth and self-awareness.

Music is a big consideration for the beginner. You may want to incorporate background music to get in the mood for meditation or to simply obscure distracting noises in other parts of your home or from outside. You may also play useful training tapes and inspirational recordings that are preliminary tools for meditation.

MEDITATION TO GO

While you should strive to establish a meditation oasis in your home for your meditation practice, it's not the only place you can meditate. You can create an impromptu meditation space wherever you are.

THE CAR

We spend a lot of time in our cars—and much of it is stressful, thanks to traffic, potholes, and long commutes. But it doesn't have to be that way. Every journey is an opportunity to practice mindfulness. You can meditate a number of ways while in your car:

Breathe. Every time you hit a red light, stop, look, and listen *to the sound of your own breath*. You can use red lights like bells as reminders to breathe deeply and be present.

Learn. Stock up on inspirational audiobooks, and listen while you drive. There are countless texts that can inspire your meditative state on the road—from popular bestselling authors such as Deepak Chopra and Pema Chödrön, to readings from the Bible, collections of haiku and Zen koans, or mystical poets, such as Rumi, St. Teresa of Avila, and William Blake.

Listen. Music can help you turn any time you spend behind the wheel into a mindful experience. While traditional chanting—from the ancient Sanskrit chants of Kirtan to Gregorian chants—is said to vibrate at sacred frequencies, any inspirational music you like may work for you as well. Choose from gospel, classical, Christian, hymns, New Age, jazz, and even rock and roll music—the choice is yours.

THE OFFICE

Wherever you work, you can find ways to incorporate meditation into your workday. If you have your own office, you can simply shut the door and tune in to your own breath whenever you feel the need to unplug from workplace intrigue. Certain icons and elements can serve as reminders and meditation aids, such as:

- *Scented spritzes* to freshen your office as you settle in, marking the difference in mood as you begin to meditate
- *Wall calendars*, with photos or images of sacred places, nature, and/ or iconography, to serve as focus points for meditation
- *Pillows*, for sitting on the floor or propping up your back if you remain seated in your chair
- *Plants*, to help improve the air quality in your room and bring you in touch with nature
- *Timers*, to schedule meditation breaks throughout the workday

Taking meditation breaks while at work will not only help you deal with any stress, anxiety, or irritability you may experience while you are there—it will improve your focus, creativity, and productivity.

Inner Smile Meditation

Practiced by Buddhists and Taoists, this meditation seems tailor made for the workplace. Whenever you feel stressed, anxious, or irritated, imagine that you are smiling inside at your forehead or your jaw or anywhere your body is holding tension. It's not as silly as it may sound; the simple act of *thinking* about smiling can trigger an upswing in mood. What's more, it's a great way to amuse yourself in long meetings.

PLANES, TRAINS, BOATS, AND BUSES

Wherever you go, there you are—meditating. You can download meditation apps for your iPhone, tune in to contemplative music on your iPod, take along inspirational books to read, or simply focus on the rhythm of the train as it hurtles along the rails, or the sound of waves as they lap against the sides of the boat, or the hum of the wheels of the bus as they go round and round.

THE GOLDEN CORD OF FLIGHT

Planes offer a unique perspective for traveling meditators. The world we live in looks different from 30,000 feet in the air. Take this opportunity to observe our planet as it really is—a small speck in an infinite universe of which you are a part. Sit by the window, and look out as the plane takes off. Imagine a golden cord running from the plane to the Earth and from the plane out into the universe. Contemplate this golden cord as the plane jets across the sky, and visualize that you, too, are part of this golden cord—a stream of pure light that reaches down through your body, into the ground, all the way to the center of the Earth and all the way up through the crown of your head into the sky and into the eternity beyond.

THE OM OF THE RAILS

Trains, with their rolling rhythm, provide a sort of built-in chant to accompany you on your journey and soothe you into a meditative state. Close your eyes, and focus on this music of the rails. See what comes up for you.

THE WHEELS OF THE BUS

Buses are a communal form of transportation that evoke memories of elementary school, summer camp, and sports activities. The next time you find yourself on a bus, focus on your favorite bus-trip memory from your childhood. Close your eyes, and while you ride, recall that happy time in as much sensory detail as possible. This may reveal what's missing in your life today—and what you need to do to make new, happy memories now.

ENLIGHTENMENT, AHOY!

Boats give us the opportunity to be on the water. In Buddhism, water represents purity, serenity, and clarity. Just being on the water can resonate with us, sending a subliminal message to rinse our minds clean. While you're on the boat, go out on the deck, look out at the water around you, and repeat to yourself: *I am the boat, I am the water, I am purity*.

YOUR BODY IN MEDITATION

You don't have to twist your body into the traditional lotus position of the yogi, sitting cross-legged on the floor, feet twisted like pretzels high on your thighs. But a few guidelines are necessary for productive and comfortable meditation.

POSTURE COUNTS

First and most important, allow your spine to be upright. Imagine it elongated, without having to strain yourself. The elongated spinal position allows for optimum breathing and proper stacking of the vertebrae. Besides a practice of proper breathing to aid circulation, the right posture ensures that the entire body can oxygenate without hindrance.

For the spine to be upright, you will either be sitting, standing, lying down, or walking for meditation practice.

SITTING MEDITATION

For now, we will focus on traditional sitting meditation. Which is best: a comfortable chair or the solid surface of the floor? Sitting postures require a firm foundation, but at the same time, enough padding should be under you to promote circulation and comfort. Few chairs can accommodate the spread of a seated person with folded knees at the sides, so the floor is a good place to begin. However, if you are not able to sit this way for any reason, a good chair will be necessary.

The second consideration is what to do with your limbs. If you are sitting on the floor, should your legs be crossed or folded? Should your feet be tucked under you or at the side? You'll need to do some experimentation here. And, just because someone you know meditates in a perfect folded-leg position doesn't mean you'll be able to do so right away. Keep in mind that circulation is more important than how your position looks. One posture you can try if cross-legged doesn't work for you is this: Kneel, and spread your knees apart so you can put a couple of stacked yoga blocks or a cushion (on its side) between your thighs. Sit down so your sitting bones are supported on the blocks or cushion and your knees are folded. You are in a supported kneeling position with your calves underneath you and perhaps slightly splayed out. Sit up tall. If you plan to sit in a chair, your feet must be supported either by the floor, a footrest, a yoga block, or a cushion.

Try sitting in several different positions. If, within five minutes, you start to feel numbness in your feet, legs, knees, or bottom, get up and move about for five minutes. Then try another sitting position. Do this until you find a position that doesn't impose any restrictions or discomfort for at least fifteen minutes at a time.

GET COMFORTABLE: YOUR HANDS

When you've found your optimum sitting position, what should you do with your hands? If your hands sweat easily, you may want to keep them open, palms up. If they get cold easily, you may want to place them downward, on your lap or knees. Another comfortable position is to place them on your tummy either folded or interlaced.

GET COMFORTABLE: YOUR EYES

Your eyes: Will they be open or closed? This is another personal preference, and it depends on the environment you've selected as your meditation space. Whether the available light helps you become still and relaxed will determine your choice. The eyes-open position is one way to begin meditation, which initially may help you avoid confusing the practice with rest or slumber. Since one of the goals is to raise awareness and harness the mind, using your eyes to notice detail, focus attention, and connect with nature is one way to start a meditation practice. You can also begin with eyes closed. Closed eyes help you bring your attention inward so you aren't stimulated by what you see. When meditating in a group, closing your eyes can help avoid the distraction of others around you.

HAVE A SEAT

The lotus is regarded as the standard sitting posture of meditation. You'll see it depicted in diagrams for the yoga student and frequently in Buddhist images from China, Tibet, and Japan. Although in the Far East and Middle East it is an accepted way of sitting, it's not as easily achieved in the West, and that can be a big deterrent when starting a meditation practice. There are variations on this posture, though, and everyone can find one that is suitable. Variations on the lotus posture are covered in the following sections, but keep in mind these caveats before you begin:

- If you choose to sit in a chair, make sure you have a sturdy but comfortable sitting chair with a tall back that will keep your spine straight and your back supported.
- Keep your feet flat on the floor or on a block, and sit up straight with your sitting bones firmly rooted into the seat of the chair. If you must lean back, make sure your lumbar spine is supported by a rolled up towel in the lower curve of the spine.
- Avoid tight clothing or footwear, furniture that pushes against your limbs, and slippery fabric covers that will interfere with comfort and relaxation.

- If you choose to be seated on the floor, make sure the surface is completely flat. Use a rug or pad on hard surfaces, followed by a seat cushion or bench that fits you while seated. Choose a posture that allows you to place your knees as close to the floor as possible so that your spine will remain upright in a beneficial position. If your knees do not reach the floor, support them with blankets or cushions so they aren't just hanging in space.
- If your back tires easily, you can lean against a wall, with your legs stretched out in front of you. Place a cushion or rolled blanket under any parts of your legs that don't rest comfortably on the floor; same goes for the curve of your lumbar spine.

For sitting meditation, the lotus posture is viewed as the ideal way to connect the body with the vital energy of earth. Like a lotus, your trunk is akin to the flower's root, grounding itself to the stabilizing force of the land. At the same time, the watery regions of thought and emotion surround you, yet the meditation process enables you to float through them unaffected.

BURMESE LOTUS

The Burmese lotus is so named because it is the sitting tradition of Southeast Asia. The legs are folded, one in front of the other, so that the calves and feet of both legs are resting on the floor. This is a good beginning posture.

HALF AND QUARTER LOTUS

For the half lotus, while seated, just one leg (whichever is more comfortable) is folded upward so that the foot rests on the opposite inner thigh. The other leg is tucked under the first. This position takes some practice.

The quarter lotus is similar to the half lotus except that, instead of resting on the thigh, one foot rests on the calf of the opposite leg. This posture is easy to negotiate.

FULL LOTUS

While seated, the legs are folded upward, with the right foot placed on the left hip and the left foot placed on the right hip. The hands rest on the knees. An advanced version of this posture is the *Baddha Padma-sana*, where the hands are crossed behind the back and the big toes on either side are grasped. Your chin is then pressed down, and your eyes are focused on the tip of the nose. This posture is not recommended for beginners.

STANDING MEDITATION

You may find yourself at a time or place where traditional sitting meditation is not possible. If that should be the case, standing meditation is quite effective, although it may not be comfortable for extended periods. Any meditation lasting less than fifteen minutes is adaptable to standing meditation.

Standing meditation is a key component of Qi Gong, the ancient Chinese system of exercise and breathing designed for wellness and peace of mind. Tai Chi is a form of Qi Gong, which in Chinese means "working with life energy."

WHEN YOUR BACK'S AGAINST THE WALL

The keys to comfortable standing meditation are standing upright and maintaining balance. If you become tired, lean your back fully against a wall. Then you can conclude the meditation session.

Stand with your feet about 12 inches apart, far enough apart to evenly balance your weight. Feel your feet supported by the earth. With your spine upright and your shoulder blades back and down, slightly tilt your chin upward without stretching your neck. This isn't a military stance; that would be tiring. Make the posture steady and sweet. Your hands may be placed with palms against your thighs. Or, you may find it more comfortable to hold both hands close to the center of your body, palms inward. Do not cross or fold your arms in standing meditation.

DEAD TO THE WORLD

Prone meditation is also called lying meditation and, in yoga, *savasana*, or the Corpse. This posture makes it possible to maintain mental and physical stillness while lying down.

Start by choosing a firm surface. If you're on the floor, make sure it is padded enough not to press against portions of the body and cause numbness. If the surface is too comfortable, such as a mattress, it may encourage lethargy and sleep. Try to find a happy medium.

Lie flat on your back. Place a cushion underneath your knees to help relax the lower back when you lie down. Do not put a cushion or pillow underneath your head or neck. Relax your head, neck, and shoulders, and allow your arms to relax, with palms open, about 6 inches away from your body. Relax your thighs, calves, and heels into the floor. Look directly up without stretching your neck in any way. If the light from the ceiling is too strong, use a floor lamp instead. You can do this with your eyes open, or close your eyes and place an eye pillow over them to block out the light. Sink into the support of the earth.

WALKING MEDITATION

Walking meditation is what it sounds like: meditation on the move. Walking meditation is different from sitting and standing meditation because you have to pay attention to your movement so you don't wander into traffic or bump into a tree. What makes this meditation similar to sitting and standing meditation is that, in all cases, you become acutely aware of your physical body and its surroundings. Walking meditation is excellent as an alternative to sitting meditation. Some people like to sit for most of their meditation session but then spend the last few minutes in walking meditation; and, for some who practice sitting meditation for longer periods of time, walking meditation periodically gets the body moving without breaking the meditative flow.

MEDITATION FOR WIGGLE WORMS

Walking meditation is a great way to enjoy walking and to reap the benefits of meditation at the same time. It's also great for people who simply refuse to sit still. Walking meditation can be a good way to ease into the meditation concept without the commitment of sitting (sitting for even five minutes is a fairly serious commitment for some people).

HOW TO PRACTICE WALKING MEDITATION

To practice walking meditation, first, decide where you will walk. You can do walking meditation outside or around a room. You should have a prepared path in mind so you don't spend time thinking about where to go during the meditation. Know exactly where you are going: around the block, to the end of the path, around the periphery of the living room, or to an outdoor labyrinth.

Begin by spending a moment focusing and breathing to center yourself and prepare for the meditation. Then, taking slow, deliberate steps, walk. As you walk, notice how your breath feels as it comes in and goes out of your body. Notice how your limbs move, how your feet feel, how your hands and arms hang, the position of your torso, your neck, your head. Don't judge yourself as you walk. Just notice.

Once you feel you've observed yourself well, begin to observe the environment around you as you walk. Don't let it engage you. If something you see sets you off on some long, involved path of thought that has nothing to do with how you feel walking through the place you are walking, then as soon as you catch your mind wandering (and it will), gently bring your thoughts back to your breathing.

While new to walking meditation, stay with your breath for a long while. Before you can start noticing and focusing on the rest of your body and your environment, you need to be able to focus on the breath. Otherwise, your mind will be all over the place.

FINDING THE RIGHT TIME TO MEDITATE

When is a good time for meditation? The diurnal (daily) clock is the one we set our conscious life to, but few are aware of the subtle forces at work each day. At sunrise, the environment is illuminated, and natural life awakens. At noon, the sun is directly overhead, with light and heat at their most intense. Midday is a vital time, and the life force is at its peak. At sunset, the light diminishes as it sinks below the horizon, and most active life begins to withdraw. The midnight hour is also a pivotal time of the day. These four periods are regarded as the "peak points" of the day—the diurnal rhythm. The peak points are when you may want to practice, but these times often conflict with other duties.

Sunrise Meditation

Some yoga texts say that the two hours before sunrise are optimum for deep meditation. If you have children, making time to meditate before they arise may prove the most practical. Not everyone is able or willing to make the switch to early-morning hours, but try it at least once. A vacation, pilgrimage, or retreat may make it possible. It also helps to make the intention to arise at a specific time just before falling asleep the night before.

Many people find it useful to start the day with a morning meditation. By clearing the mind and consciously experiencing stillness, the day does not seem so daunting or ordinary—whichever the case may be. Similarly, an early-evening meditation clears the mind of the day's events.

Whatever time you find best fits your schedule, try to keep it between mealtimes. If you have not eaten for several hours, a growling stomach may interrupt your session. And, if you're meditating right after a meal, the digestive process could be disruptive. Also, sitting for an extended period right after eating tends to compress the esophagus, bringing on acid reflux or heartburn. Choose a time that is not directly after you've eaten or when you are hungry.

KNOWING HOW LONG TO MEDITATE

Depending on the meditation system in question, guidelines on the length of a session conflict, so in the beginning it's up to you to decide. Some recommend forty-five minutes; others say that twenty minutes is enough of a meditation break to make a difference. But, even five minutes can make all the difference on a stressful day.

That said, if day after day you find yourself squeezing meditation in between daily responsibilities, you aren't allowing enough time for a good practice. Waking up an extra fifteen minutes early could remedy that or moving errands to just one part of the day instead of scattering them throughout the day could ease up on the time crunch.

Setting a timer or placing a clock in your meditation space may be useful in the beginning, but you don't want the clock to rule your session. In fact, the passage of time is always monitored by the subconscious mind. In meditation, this awareness often comes forward. So, set yourself up mentally for a fifteen-minute meditation session, and stop when you think you've achieved it. If you don't suceed, try again the next time you have a session. Since meditation is a process of becoming aware, the passage of time will make itself known soon enough. Remember, you are leaving the world of schedules and moving into the timeless. Another way to release the mind from time concerns is to buy a meditation timer. That way, you can set the timer, and its gentle "ding" will tell you when your time is up.

Remember, this is a commitment to only yourself and not to any other person or long-term goal. It's a gift of time that you are investing in your well-being. So, take five whenever you can.

THE ONE-BREATH MEDITATION

Everyday life continually poses challenges to our inner peace. In the midst of a stressful episode, whether at home or at work, we often long for the peaceful moments that a secluded, quiet meditation offers. But the real world doesn't offer such moments when they're most needed. We have to create them. At these times, a conscious pause can refresh the body and mind just as well as an extended meditation session. All that's needed is the desire to stop and take action or no action, as the case may be.

If you find yourself at a standstill at work, feeling that you've come to the end of the rope you're climbing, stop. Remind yourself that this is an opportune time for momentary meditation to refresh and relax your mind from the climb. Pause all thoughts, and remind yourself that your inner peace prevails at this moment. Think of that peace as a place within you. Straighten your spine as you do this, lift your chin slightly upward and broaden your chest. Focus your eyes above your head, at the ceiling or wall. Slowly and deliberately take a conscious breath. Think of your place of peace opening its door as the air fills your lungs. On exhaling, appreciate the moment for allowing you to pause, and return to the work at hand.

Take Five

In the beginning, you may want to start with exercises that last five to ten minutes and build a longer practice from there. Don't pressure yourself or set unrealistic goals. Just stay with your program, and you'll see progress. Once you have decided on how long you'll meditate, you'll more quickly notice results if you commit to consistently follow your practice. There may be times when this is not possible, but this steady meditation practice gives you the groundwork you need to be able to meditate at any time and in any place.

CHAPTER 4
DON'T THINK, BREATHE!

"How can you ever know anything if you are too busy thinking?"

—BUDDHA

Meditation begins with a very simple premise—focusing your attention on a single point. It trains the overactive mind to slow its frenetic pace and hold awareness still. The focus of meditation could be the breath, a sound, or an image, but, no matter the focal point, the goal is to quiet the mind.

REIN IN YOUR THOUGHTS AND FEELINGS

Once you begin to focus your attention, a host of interesting situations—in the realm of thoughts and feelings—present themselves. Thoughts and feelings are important considerations in the early stages of meditation. As soon as you establish your time and space and start your first sessions, you may become aware that thoughts and feelings begin to rush forward for your attention. Everything you may have put on the back burner comes forward, seeking attention or resolution.

THE BACK BURNER METHOD

Instead of trying to push thoughts out of the way, you could make a meditation of viewing them in a detached, disengaged manner. You can do this by neutralizing them. Here's how it works: If a distracting thought comes forward, welcome it and ask it to put its case before you. Then listen to what it communicates and return it to the back burner. Do not personify the thought; view it as a disembodied object, like a bubble or cloud. Consider what the thought communicated to you for only a moment, giving it a minimal amount of time, and allow the next thought to come forward.

For example, you are meditating, and the thought comes to your mind that you didn't shop for dinner. Ordinarily, you might think of a quick menu, the items you'll need, and if they're not in the kitchen, where to buy them. That might lead to remembering that your checkbook is at the office so you'll have to use the credit card, and the bill arrived yesterday.

> *"That's what I call meditation. You simply stand aloof and just see the mind disappearing, like a cloud on a faraway horizon, leaving the sky clean and pure. And in that state arises your consciousness in its full glory, in its full celebration."*
>
> —OSHO

Instead, you neutralize the thought by acknowledging that dinner wasn't included in today's planning. Tell the thought you will plan it when your meditation is over. Give the thought your attention, assign it a place, and move on.

WATCH THAT ATTITUDE

Feelings are a different matter, arising from another realm of our being. Emotions are not appeased by logic; they possess a stream of action all their own. We can visualize thought as linear and emotion as circular. Thus, we cannot reason with feelings. The impressions we receive from feelings, however, do not have to affect our awareness.

Feelings may come through the body as sensations, pleasant or unpleasant. They may also appear as attitudes, especially toward yourself. For example, as you begin to sit in meditation, you feel restless, saying to yourself, "Okay, let's get down to business." What does this mean?

Initially, you may feel a wave of impatience because you procrastinated throughout the day and it's weighing on you. Then you may feel a wave of frustration, as you're reminded that there doesn't seem to be enough time to do everything you want. And, finally, a sense of anger may well up because the interference of others has taken up so much of your time.

Try addressing the impatience with humor: "What's the hurry? I'm here to be free of business." Meet the frustration with calm: "The time I give myself will multiply the time I can give to everything else." Neutralize anger with kindness: "I have been inconvenienced by the interference of others, and now I can make it up to myself."

Too Many Thoughts, Too Little Time

Most of us think between 50,000 and 75,000 thoughts a day—up to 50,000 of which we also thought yesterday and the day before. Meditation helps us clear out the redundancies that clutter our minds—leaving space for new insights.

Other feelings may appear when you begin to meditate (for example, hopelessness, discouragement, and other counterproductive feelings). What would you say to a close friend who expressed those feelings to you? You would undoubtedly extend words of hope, encouragement, and motivation. Now, support yourself as you would support your friends.

Countering emotions is not the aim here, as that can be conflicting. The goal is to balance and settle the emotions—and that is not a quick, easy task. You will need much practice at this because you are probably harder on yourself than anyone else. One attitude to always keep throughout this process is what the Buddhists call loving-kindness. You must practice it on yourself in the beginning. Allow it to become the byword during all the time you spend in meditation, and allow it to flood into all aspects of your life.

THOUGHTS VERSUS FEELINGS

Thought and feeling can take their turns in sessions. Devote one session to thought, the next to feeling. You may alternate each time you sit for a meditation. As you continue this pattern, an interesting phenomenon begins to happen. The rush of thoughts and feelings subside, and you begin to notice that something else is present—your own awareness, anticipating the next thought or feeling. At that moment, there is a pause in thought and feeling, and it is that pause that you are seeking to cultivate. That is meditation.

The Anchor of Mindfulness

All forms of meditation have many teachings and goals in common: to be in the moment, to establish a distance between yourself and your thoughts and feelings, and to become, metaphorically, the anchor. The rest of you is the ship, and your surroundings are the sea.

Asking questions is a beneficial exercise in noticing thoughts and feelings through meditation. This is not a process of analyzing. Rather, it is a way of exercising mindfulness. And, throughout the process, you are also bringing forth another innate ability: insight. Together, these can provide you with honest, clear answers to all the questions you may have about yourself and your life in general—from "Why can't I let that resentment go?" to "If I could change careers, what would I do?"

HOUSEKEEPING FOR YOUR BRAIN

While you are in meditation, thoughts and feelings present themselves. Don't let them fly away; catch them—like butterflies—and ask the following questions:

- Why do I think/feel this way about that person or situation?
- What causes led to this thought/feeling?
- Why do I still think/feel this way about that person or situation?
- What conditions could make this thought/feeling change?

This is an exercise in "mental housecleaning." And, like regular house-cleaning, you can observe yourself doing it. Layers of awareness unfold like the proverbial lotus, and you experience insights along the way.

THE SEED MEDITATION

Essentially, there are two basic ways to meditate: "with seed" and "without seed." These are generic terms, and just about every type of meditation will fall into one of these two approaches.

MEDITATION WITH SEED

What is meditation with seed? Here, you use a single image, word, or sound to focus the mind in order to reach the launching point away from ordinary mental activity. In some religious traditions, certain prayers serve as seed meditations. They can be quite extensive, and the entire meditation practice may be based on recitation or the silent reading of prayers or revered writings. In others, words of power or mantras are repeated at length to attain the launching point. These may be short or long; they may be repeated several times or just once to arouse or stimulate the mind to reach the launching point.

Seed meditation can also direct your focus to images or sounds. The visual and auditory concentration helps you stay within a theme or atmosphere of meditation. Some traditions emphasize this through meditation or prayer with statues, illustrations, and architectural design. Others use music, sounds with bells or drums, chants, and spoken prayers.

5-MINUTE SEED MEDITATION

You can choose a seed for your meditation practice anywhere, anytime. Whether you're at home, at the office, in your car, or out in nature, you can find the right seed for even the most impromptu meditation.

Just look around you:
- A tree
- A star in the sky
- The sound of waves breaking on the beach
- A statue of the Buddha
- A saint's medal
- A Celtic cross, Star of David, or other religious symbol
- A landscape photo or illustration

Just look within you:
- A favorite prayer
- The sound of "Om"
- A personal intention
- A quality you wish to develop in yourself
- A favorite memory
- A mentor or spiritual leader

THE SANS SEED MEDITATION
Meditation without seed is another technique. Here, the goal is twofold:

1. Empty the mind
2. Still the senses

This can be accomplished through silence, separation from familiar surroundings, and eliminating all but the basic necessities of daily existence. Monastic life and retreats are an example of this type of meditation tradition.

THE BENEFITS OF SEED AND SANS SEED
Either approach—with or without seed—is quite effective, depending on the circumstances and the practitioner. The advantage of seed meditation is that it allows the familiar to become so familiar that we no longer even think about it. In fact, we are released from thinking altogether. The

advantage of meditation without seed is that it dispenses with the tendency to focus on familiar things so we can explore other realities.

The use of seed meditation is expressed in a number of modern paths, although it is called by other names. It may be referred to as intentional meditation, where specific goals are formulated and the meditation experience is aimed toward those ends. Meditation without seed is also referred to as choiceless meditation, a term coined by Jiddu Krishnamurti, a twentieth-century philosopher and proponent of self-discovery through meditation.

The analogy of a seed is most appropriate. It alludes to the "unfolding" of the conscious mind to reach enlightenment, just as a seed grows to a flower and unfolds its splendid petals to reveal a perfect design. At the same time, a seed resides within the mature plant, indicating that another flower, or level, awaits unfolding in the future.

THE RIGHT WAY TO BREATHE

Have you ever listened to your breathing? Or observed your rhythm of inhaling and exhaling? Most people who do so find that they breathe in short breaths that do not completely fill the lungs. Once they notice, they start to take deeper breaths. The infusion of oxygen by this exercise can bring on a "high" of sorts, but after a while they forget the deep breathing and go off to their regular activities, with unmonitored, shallow breathing.

Of course, we take air into the body through the nose and mouth. But, meditation masters say that the "center" where we are drawing in the air should not be in our nostrils, or throat, or even the lungs. Rather, we should breathe in from the stomach, the way babies breathe—with our bellies.

JUST BREATHE

If you are ready to pursue the goal of a personal meditation practice, then getting started with some exercises can set the foundation for your regimen right away. Let's start—as most meditation training starts—with breathing.

You may wonder why breathing is a central component in meditation and why it is emphasized so much. After all, breath is a natural, autonomic function of the body. But, that's why it's so important. When the body is completely at rest, breathing becomes quite noticeable—at times, it even intrudes into awareness of the present. Centuries ago, the rhythm, strength, and energetic exchange of breath with the body was recognized as the ideal timekeeper and modulator. There's no escaping it, and there's every reason to consciously and optimally breathe because it contributes so much to physical and mental relaxation. Needless to say, you should use good breathing habits, which you can promote with a few warm-up exercises.

STAND UP TO YOUR BREATH

Stand with your feet slightly apart to balance your weight. Focus on only your breathing for three minutes.

Now take three "good" breaths, not necessarily deep or long, but comfortably fill your lungs as you inhale and exhale. As you take in each breath, feel your strong legs supporting you, and hold your abdomen in for support. Raise your arms; then lower them as you exhale. While inhaling, think of the air also entering your body, from the ground upward to your head. Try to allow each breath equal time in duration and quality. And, try to keep the rhythm the same as your "normal" breathing, especially in the beginning.

SIT DOWN AND BREATHE

Sit in a comfortable chair, making sure that you are as upright as possible and your feet are comfortably on the floor. Place your hands on your lap or palms down on your thighs. Focus on only your breathing for three minutes. Do not attempt to control or direct your breath; just observe it.

Next, lower your chin to your chest, and inhale while slowly raising your head. As you exhale, lower your chin back to your chest. Do this for three "good" breaths. Try to do it as slowly as possible.

WARM UP YOUR BODY

Physical sensation is one of the first things you will become aware of in meditation. When they are not in motion, your senses are directed inward rather than outward, and you will notice things that may not have been apparent at other times. Therefore, you need to relax physically as much as possible before a meditation session so you aren't distracted by body stress.

FLAT ON YOUR BACK SPINAL WARM-UP

To help the spine maintain a natural, upright position, start with a gentle spine warm-up. Lie down on the floor on your stomach, face turned to the side. Take three relaxed breaths. Then, with your hands on either side of you pushing against the floor, exhale and gently lift your head, shoulders, and chest off the floor, pressing your pelvis into the earth and carefully arching your spine. Broaden your chest slowly, turning your head forward and stretching your chin toward the ceiling if that feels comfortable to you. Don't force your head, neck, shoulders, or back into a strenuous stretch or lift your torso for an extended period. Exhale, and lower yourself back to the floor and take another three relaxed breaths.

LONG LEG WARM-UP

Sitting for an extended period can be difficult if you are not accustomed to it. As you work on sitting for longer periods of time, warm up your legs at predetermined intervals to encourage proper circulation. This warm-up also helps strengthen the lower vertebrae in the back.

Lie down on the floor, on your back, arms at your side, and palms downward. Take three relaxed breaths. On the third inhale, lift one leg;

bend it, bringing the knee toward your chest. Use both hands to grasp your bent leg, and bring it as close to your chest as comfort allows. Take three relaxed breaths, and on the third exhale, release your bent leg and allow it to return to the floor. After allowing a minute for integration, repeat the posture with the other leg.

TAKE IT EASY

Go slowly. Don't set any specific goals or expectations. It's still too early for that.

Mindfulness is a process. As you build time for more meditation into your life and sprinkle more 5-minute mindfulness breaks into your schedule, you'll grow more comfortable with the process—and experience more of the benefits.

MONKEY MIND, BEGINNER'S MIND

Congratulations, you've learned how to use one of the most powerful tools in the mindfulness arsenal: meditation.

It's not easy to quiet your monkey mind, but you are on your way. Remember, meditation is a practice. It requires time and patience and, most of all, dedication.

Practice makes perfect—and in this case, the perfection you seek already resides within.

"A quiet mind cureth all."

—ROBERT BURTON

CHAPTER 5
STRESS RELIEF FOR YOUR BODY

"Hallow the body as a temple."

—Khalil Gibran

You've only got one body, and it carries you around all your life. Yet, few of us treat our own flesh and blood with the love and respect it deserves. When our body suffers, our mind suffers as well—and mindfulness eludes us. If we are to be truly mindful, we need to listen to our body and hear what it is trying to tell us. Failure to do so endangers our physical health and ultimately our mental and emotional health.

How good are you to your body?
1. **Every night, you sleep an average of:**
   A. Seven and a half hours or more
   B. Six to seven hours
   C. Four to six hours
   D. Sleep? Who needs sleep?

2. **When you're stressed out, you:**
   A. Go to yoga class
   B. Take a walk
   C. Eat too much chocolate
   D. Drink too much wine

3. **Your idea of a good meal is:**
   A. Brown rice and beans
   B. Sushi

C. A Big Mac

D. A martini

4. You get a massage:

A. Once a week

B. Once a month

C. When you're on vacation

D. You've never had a massage

5. You weigh:

A. What you weighed in high school

B. Fifteen pounds more than you should

C. Thirty pounds more than you should

D. Fifty or more pounds than you should

6. You think of yourself as:

A. An athlete

B. More physically active than most

C. Not as physically active as you should be

D. A couch potato and proud of it

7. Your favorite part of yoga class is:

A. Savasana

B. Vinyasa flow

C. Deep breathing

D. You've never been to a yoga class

8. You have studied:

A. Yoga

B. Tai Chi

C. Martial arts

D. None of the above

9. You suffer from:

A. No major ailments

B. High blood pressure

C. Obesity

D. Diabetes

10. You exercise:

A. Three to five times a week

B. Twice a week

C. Once a month

D. Rarely

11. You have sex:

A. As often as possible

B. Three times a week

C. Once a month if you're lucky

D. Never—sex is overrated

12. You practice deep breathing exercises:

A. Every day

B. Three times a week

C. When you feel really stressed out

D. Never

13. Your eating habits could be described as:

A. Vegan/Vegetarian

B. Lean protein, fruits and veggies, complex carbs

C. Gourmet

D. Junk-food heaven

Now tally up your score.

- *If you checked mostly As*, you take relatively good care of your body, but with a better understanding of mindfulness, you can substantially boost your health and well-being.

- *If you checked mostly Bs*, you do pay some attention to self-care but not as much nor as deeply as you could if you were to use the tools of mindfulness to maximize every opportunity for good health.
- *If you checked mostly Cs*, you are not giving your body the nurturing it deserves. You need to nurture yourself, which in turn will nurture your physical and emotional well-being.
- *If you checked mostly Ds*, you have neglected your body—to the detriment of your health. Mindfulness can help you learn to listen to your body and give it what it needs—and not only improve your well-being but transform your life in the process.

Your body is a miraculous collection of cells that works together to create a unique human being—you. That uniqueness even extends to stress and its effects on your body.

Stress manifests itself in any number of ways, depending on your individual makeup and the situation. You may experience:

Migraines after a hard day at work
Abdominal cramps three days after the car breaks down
Irritable bowel whenever your family comes to visit
Panic attacks before final exams
Nightmares for months after a divorce

Stress can literally cause us pain, make us sick, even kill us. That's why it's critical to learn how your body responds to stress—and act accordingly.

SIDE EFFECTS OF STRESS

You already know you're not a superhero. Stress takes its toll on your body, with any of the following unwanted side effects:

- Sweating
- Cold extremities
- Nausea, vomiting
- Diarrhea
- Muscle tension
- Dry mouth

- Confusion
- Nervousness, anxiety
- Irritability, impatience
- Frustration
- Panic
- Hostility, aggression

Even worse, being under stress for extended periods has been linked to depression, loss of or increased appetite, resulting in undesirable weight changes, frequent minor illnesses, increased aches and pains, sexual problems, fatigue, loss of interest in social activities, increased addictive behavior, chronic headaches, acne, chronic backaches, chronic stomachaches, and worsened symptoms associated with medical conditions such as asthma and arthritis. Let's take a closer look at some of the most common ways stress can manifest in our bodies.

BRAIN BURNOUT

The burnout epidemic is a result of people failing to manage their stress. Many people struggle with anxiety and depression, both signs that the brain's circuits are not firing properly. Two mental illnesses—generalized anxiety disorder and depression—exemplify a brain short-circuiting. Generalized anxiety disorder is chronic stress for no apparent reason, while depression is a sense of empty hopelessness and a loss of the ability to enjoy life. Both exemplify a brain on burnout that can't tell what's really stressful or even what's pleasurable anymore. If you have experienced either condition, reflect on your life and see if a stressful event, job, or relationship may have been a factor contributing to this condition.

THE BRAIN SOOTHER

When your mind is overburdened, do something with your hands. Many people find relief in baking bread, painting, gardening, doing home repairs, or practicing amateur carpentry. Building or creating something helps the mind to focus. When you are hammering a birdhouse together or decorating a birthday cake, you don't have room in your brain to worry.

TUMMY TROUBLE

Stress doesn't just affect the brain; it also affects the digestive system, or "second brain." The gut is the source of hormones and chemicals that regulates mood. Long-term episodic or chronic stress has been linked to a number of digestive maladies. It's no wonder that stress-related conditions, such as irritable bowel syndrome, Crohn's disease, and celiac disease, are on the rise as people's guts struggle with stress overload.

HOW STRESS AFFECTS THE DIGESTIVE SYSTEM

When the body undergoes the stress response, first, the blood is diverted away from the digestive tract to large muscles. The stomach and intestines may empty their contents, preparing the body for quick action. Many people experiencing stress, anxiety, and nervousness also experience stomach cramps, nausea, vomiting, or diarrhea. (Doctors used to call this a "nervous stomach.")

YOU ARE WHAT YOU EAT

Poor diet is also a contributor to digestive distress. Many people forget to drink water and eat well while stressed, which can lead to constipation and even hemorrhoids. Others substitute soda and processed food when life gets tough, and both can cause constipation from lack of fiber and essential nutrients. To maintain a healthy digestive system, be sure to eat well and drink plenty of water, especially when stressed.

THE TUMMY SOOTHER

If you are subject to stomach upset, try one of the following fixes:

Water. Dehydration can contribute to tummy troubles, so be sure to drink lots of water—especially if you consume carbonated beverages on a regular basis.

Ginger. In Asia, ginger has long been used as a cure for gastrointestinal problems, and more people in the West are finding it helpful now as well. You can sip water and suck on some dried ginger; if that's too much for you, try hot ginger tea with honey.

Crackers. The common cure for morning sickness can also work for you whether you are pregnant or not, as the crackers help absorb some of the stomach acid that fuels upset.

Tea. In addition to ginger tea, chamomile tea and peppermint tea with honey can also help.

EMOTIONAL EATING AND STRESS SNACKING

Mood eating can lead to weight gain, in addition to digestive problems. Eating to "feel" better is not good, for your feelings or for your waistline. Yet, many people grab a soda or eat a tasty, high-fat meal to unwind after a stressful day. To make matters worse, many people have a favorite comfort food, sweet or salty, that they hold close like a teddy bear during times of stress. Even people who eat well as a rule break down for a treat in the midst of stress.

THE SNACK ATTACK SOOTHER

An occasional treat is part of a healthy and balanced diet. Eating badly to feel better, however, is neither healthy nor balanced. Explore other activities to unwind besides eating a mixing bowl of ice cream. Exercise, a healthy snack, or other treat can easily be substituted for a fatty, sugary feel-good friend as a reward for a stressful event or conversation.

THE STRESSED-OUT HEART

Heart attacks used to be an epidemic for men, the strong, silent types, who bore the stress of work and family alone. In recent years, heart attacks have become an epidemic for women, too.

THE HEARTBEAT OF STRESS

Some scientists believe stress contributes to hypertension (high blood pressure), and, for decades, people have advised the nervous, anxious, irritable, or pessimistic among them that they'll work themselves into a heart attack. In fact, people who are more likely to see events as stressful do seem to have an increased rate of heart disease. If you are one of these people, your perception of stress is about to change. Remember, you control your level of stress. Stress only controls you if you let it.

A high-fat, high-sugar, low-fiber diet (the fast-food, junk-food syndrome) contributes to fat in the blood and, eventually, a clogged, heart-attack-prone heart. Coupled with lack of exercise, the risk factors for heart disease increase, all because you were too stressed out to eat a salad and go for that walk (day after day after day).

THE HEART SOOTHER

Polluting your body with too much saturated fat and highly processed, low-fiber food has a direct effect on health. Just as a polluted river soon cleans itself when the pollution stops, so will your coronary arteries begin to clear out if the body is freed from having to process foods that are damaging to good health. So, lose the junk food, and incorporate more fruits and vegetables into your diet.

STRESSED-OUT SKIN

Ever notice how pimples get worse after a stressful presentation, a pallid complexion results in anticipation of a difficult conversation, or the lips get dry after forgetting to drink enough water? The skin, the largest organ of the human body, also shows signs of stress.

ACNE—NOT JUST FOR TEENS

Teens aren't the only ones suffering from stress-induced acne, however. Skin problems such as acne are usually related to hormonal fluctuations, which in turn can be exacerbated by stress. Stress can extend the length of time these skin flare-ups occur, and damage can take longer to repair in a compromised, stressed-out immune system.

THE SKIN SOOTHER

Try cucumber slices on your eyes after applying a facial mask or aftershave for an in-home spa experience. Dim the lights, light some candles, lie down flat, and enjoy the cucumber's coolness sinking into your skin. Now, this is refreshing! Try slightly damp, used tea bags, a chilled eye mask, or smooth stones as variations.

PIMPLED SKIN

Long-term stress can lead to chronic acne. Eating badly, forgetting to practice healthy skin care, and chronic dehydration will also affect your skin. Stress also contributes to psoriasis, hives, and other forms of dermatitis.

CHRONIC PAIN

Ever notice how migraines, arthritis, fibromyalgia, multiple sclerosis, degenerative bone and joint diseases, and old injuries all feel worse when you're under stress? That's because, along with stress's other victims, the body's pain tolerance has also succumbed.

Pain is tricky. Pain is your body's way of alerting you that something is not functioning well or is in danger and needs your attention. How much pain you have is not always directly proportional to the health risk you are facing. How you react to the pain is one factor that can make it worse. For example, a woman hospitalized for back surgery with an angry daughter in her room yelling about the hospital bill is likely to have greater and longer-lasting pain than the same woman in a room with a caring friend or nurse.

THE PAIN SOOTHER

When your mind is relaxed, it will be easier to reduce your pain than it will be if you cannot relax. Being aware that stress is exacerbating a preexisting condition is the first step to saying no to stress. A simple note to self—"This is just the mind worrying. I can handle this"—and taking several deep, relaxing breaths may decrease the pain because you will not stay in the mind-set of fear.

STRESS AND YOUR IMMUNE SYSTEM

Ever notice how a bout with a bug often follows a stressful event? Your immune system is your body's frontline defense against colds, flu, and any type of infection or illness. But when stress exhausts your body, your immune system is compromised.

THE IMMUNE SYSTEM SOOTHER

One of the best things you can do to boost your immune system is increase your beta-carotene intake. Make sure you eat plenty of sweet potatoes, carrots, spinach, cantaloupe, kale, turnip greens, papaya, broccoli, apricots, mangoes, peaches, and butternut squash. Note: Smokers and people exposed to asbestos should avoid beta-carotene.

The Stress List Exercise

Make a list of the physical symptoms you experience from excessive stress. Take the time to reflect on each physical symptom, and in the following week, be attentive to any event that triggers the physical symptom. Explore ways to minimize the stress causing the physical condition. For example, do you have headaches as a consequence of fighting with your partner over not spending enough time together? Hire a babysitter for a date night. Your body may just thank you.

THE STRESS–DISEASE CONNECTION

While not every expert agrees on which diseases are linked to stress and which to other factors, such as bacteria or genetics, an increasing number of scientists and others believe that the interrelatedness of the body and mind means that mental and emotional stress can contribute to, if not cause, almost any physical problem. Because of this interconnectedness, the cause and effect can occur in the reverse direction, too: Physical illness and injury can contribute to mental and emotional stress.

The result is a spiral of stress—disease—more stress—more disease, which can ultimately cause serious damage to the body, mind, and spirit. The question of which came first may be irrelevant, and quibbling about which conditions are caused by stress and which are not may be irrelevant as well. Managing stress, whether it caused physical problems or resulted from them, will put the body into a more balanced state, and a body that is more balanced is in a better position to heal itself. It will also help the mind to deal with physical injury or illness, thereby reducing suffering.

DISARM YOUR BULLYING MIND

Stress cannot ravage your body unless you let it. Your mind, the command center of your body and spirit, is more than just the brain in your head. How you perceive the world is key to what causes you stress. Is life really too busy? Are you juggling too many things? Control your mind with self-awareness and practice stress-busting in daily life, and you are well on your way to controlling stress.

RUNNING ON AUTOPILOT

Everyone knows what it's like to run on autopilot. Those are the days when you don't even have time to sit down for all three meals, let alone take some time out for yourself. Why is there so much to do? First you're bouncing from meeting to meal to meeting, barely there; then someone says something offensive, and then the boss spills hot coffee on you, and suddenly you're descending in the dreaded roller coaster. How did that happen?

Though you may indeed have a busy job, needy family, social obligations, countless errands, and a home to maintain, who doesn't? How do some people avoid the stress roller coaster and others don't? Here's the trick: Turn off the autopilot.

Awareness is key to stopping stress before it manages you. When you put your life on autopilot, you check your brain at the door.

WHY YOUR PERCEPTION OF STRESS MATTERS

A busy day for one person is a slow day for another. Perception is key to stopping stress before it stops you. The term *perception* simply means how you see the world. A tour at the local art gallery might be inspiring for you but torture for someone who'd rather be playing paintball. It's all about perception.

Changing your perception can be challenging: That's why some people spend a lifetime in therapy with gifted professionals trying to change their perception of the world. Indeed, the whole discipline of psychology is based on how the human mind perceives the world around it.

How you see the world directly affects how you see stress. Mindfulness can help you change your perception of both.

Top Three Torments Exercise

Stop right now, and write down the first three things that you hate doing that come to mind. Does it stress you out having to deal with these things? How much do you find yourself thinking about doing these things—or *not* doing them? How important is it that you actually do them? Can you hire someone else to do them? Enlist the help of friends or family? What would it take to cross them off your list—forever?

If you're afraid of stress or have no clue what stresses you out or why, you're much more likely to become stressed than someone who knows that stress is a part of life and manages stress with meditation, exercise, or positive affirmations.

RECLAIM YOUR TIME

Remember, your mind is the command center of your body and brain. You, and only you, have the power to say, "I'm going to actually take both of my breaks today," or "I'm going to go to yoga class tonight," or "I'm going to eat dinner sitting down for a change and actually chew." Knowing all the side effects of stress controlling your life — headaches, lost sleep, fights with family, poor diet, and increased risk of disease — how can you afford not to have time for yourself?

5-MINUTE TIME-OUT EXERCISE

Make a list of the top ten things you're always planning to do for yourself but never make the time to do: get a massage, set up a meditation space, take a watercolor class, see a foreign film, whatever. Write each one down on a scrap of paper, and place the scraps in a bowl. Now close your eyes, pull one out, and do it. *Today.*

Do this every day for ten days — and see how your attitude toward time, self-care, and stress changes.

MULTITASKING: GOOD OR BAD?

If balancing the phone in one arm and a child in the other while nudging the dog away from the cat with your spare foot sounds like a slow day, you are one of the many people who multitask. Simply put, you are juggling multiple responsibilities at once, working all the time to keep control of family, work, friends, your health, your finances, and every other part of your life. In any given instant, your mind is bouncing back and forth, thinking, planning, and masterminding your life.

Multitasking is good when it helps you meet all your responsibilities. But multitasking is bad when it proves too stressful.

Some people thrive on being busy, and others struggle. Some people love doing two or three things at once, while others focus on one task at a time and cross each one off the list in its turn. No matter what your style, you need to be able to recognize when you've taken multitasking too far.

If any of these are true in your life, you may need to cut back on multitasking:

- A stressor, illness, family problem, or financial disaster zaps energy needed to manage life
- You take on a new responsibility, when you're already stretched too thin
- A person or event hijacks you in the midst of your responsibilities, preventing you from doing what needs to be done
- Any area of life explodes into an emergency: a child goes to the hospital, your job is cut to part-time, your car dies

Mindfulness can help you recognize the warning signs that you're trying to juggle too much and you need to respond accordingly.

THE BROWNOUT TEST

Ever notice how your computer slows down when it's overloaded? Whether it's loading a massive file, needs a backup, or has one too many photo albums, an overloaded computer is not the efficient, responsive tool the person with a deadline needs.

Your mind, the body's and brain's command center, also slows down under pressure. Like that stalling computer screen, the mind too experiences system errors. With care and attention, a system error can be fixed. With neglect and added stress, a system error can deteriorate into a system failure.

Stop and reflect—what are the signs of brownout in your life?

Compare your own signs of brownout with the list below. How many apply to you now?

- ❏ Waking up exhausted on a full night's sleep
- ❏ New aches and pains
- ❏ Inability to follow normal conversation
- ❏ Forgetting to eat due to lack of hunger
- ❏ Weight gain due to excessive hunger
- ❏ Nightmares or recurring dreams involving stressful situations
- ❏ Lack of emotion
- ❏ Excessive emotion
- ❏ Staring blankly at a computer screen or into space with no idea what you were thinking of
- ❏ Little interest in people, events, and activities that used to be fun
- ❏ Little desire for sex or impotence once sex is initiated
- ❏ Existing health conditions worsen

If you are experiencing five or more of these symptoms, you are browning out. It's time to take some steps to manage your stress now.

"Your sacred space is where you can find yourself again and again."

— JOSEPH CAMPBELL

CHAPTER 6

MINDFUL BODY, LUMINOUS BODY

"This very body that we have, that's sitting right here right now . . . with its aches and its pleasures . . . is exactly what we need to be fully human, fully awake, fully alive."

— PEMA CHÖDRÖN

Mindfulness can mean the difference between a stressed-out body and a luminous body.

Mindfulness helps to intimately reconnect you with your body and give it your complete attention. When you rejuvenate, care for, and nurture your body at the deepest levels, you also quiet and focus your mind, relieve tension, increase your self-knowledge and awareness, improve your quality of life, and change how you see the world.

THE UNITING OF BODY, MIND, AND SPIRIT

The mindfulness tool we use to accomplish all this is yoga. If you think yoga is just exercise requiring you to twist your body into impossible pretzels, think again. The word *yoga* comes from the ancient Sanskrit meaning, literally, "to yoke or join." Yoga traces its origins back thousands of years to India, where it began as a means of communing with the divine. This eight-limbed system — of which the "pretzel" postures are only one — is designed to encourage this communion through a combination of philosophy, postures, deep breathing, and meditation. (In fact, the postures were originally conceived to prepare the body for sitting in meditation.)

Through the practice of yoga, you can reconnect your body and mind and discover your spirit. Yoga is the art of listening to all parts of yourself—allowing you to become whole.

Working with the body through yoga connects you with spirit while unraveling the emotional, physical, and mental knots that bind you and blind you from your true nature. This process allows your essence to shine through and illuminates your entire being.

TRANSFORM YOURSELF

Yoga is a powerful, holistic, transformational tool that calms and focuses the mind and develops innate intelligence and awareness. The postures, breath awareness, and relaxation techniques develop your natural intuitive intelligence and help your mind to focus on one thing at a time instead of jumping around like a hyper monkey. When the mind is focused, the nervous, circulatory, and respiratory systems respond by slowing down. The body and mind start to relax. You feel calmer, think more clearly, and feel centered and grounded. Over time, the mind and the intelligence are able to spread throughout the body, focusing on many points at one time.

As the mind quiets, the body opens to release unnecessary tension and long-held emotions. The emotions become balanced and moderate. The body develops balanced strength, flexibility, and a stable core. You experience emotional equanimity and poise, like a tree that sways in the breeze but always come back to center. Life will always have its sunny days and stormy, windy times; with yoga you can create a strong foundation with which you can endure life's unpredictable weather.

HEAL YOURSELF

Yoga is also a therapeutic tool. Specific postures and breathing practices can relieve many ailments and disorders. Often, people are amazed to find their backaches, headaches, and joint pain will disappear with regular practice. People with cancer, cardiac problems, and multiple sclerosis can experience relief of some symptoms and develop the ability to more fully relax and cope with stress.

Everyone can embark on the yogic path regardless of age, size, flexibility, or health. Many people unfamiliar with yoga think that they have to be like a Gumby toy—able to touch their toes to their nose—but this is not true. Yoga is the great equalizer. Two people can walk into a yoga class, one very flexible with no strength and the other stiff (too strong) with little flexibility. These individuals can do the same poses, with mindfulness and care, and the overly flexible person will build strength and the stiff person will create space in his/her body. With modifications to the postures, overweight people, pregnant women, and older people can practice yoga and receive its benefits. Many types of yoga are suitable for anyone, and poses can *always* be modified to fit an individual's needs.

MINDFULNESS IN MOTION

Yoga is a process of learning to recognize and observe the reactions and habitual patterns of the mind, body, and breath. When you become aware of your patterns, you can slowly, with diligence, exchange them for new, more balanced patterns of movement, breathing, and thinking—in a word, mindfulness.

Learning yoga is like learning a new language for your body, mind, and spirit. This is why yoga is described as a practice—you practice it to gain experience and self-knowledge from your efforts.

YOUR MINDFUL BODY

When you practice yoga, you are striving to align the bones, joints, and muscles, thereby enhancing strength and flexibility, balanced muscle action, and stamina and endurance. The more you practice, the sooner you will discover the right balance between ease and effort in the poses. Once you find that balance, you'll be properly lengthening and contracting your muscle groups, stacking and feeding your bones into the joints, and soothing your nervous system. Voilà—mindfulness in motion!

How much you practice is up to you. Like meditation, the more consistent you are, the better. And, by establishing a regular practice—be it a weekly yoga class, a video you do on your own twice a week, or a daily practice you set up at home—you set the foundation you need to access the same benefits you experience during yoga practice while you're going about the rest of your day, no matter how crazy busy your day may be.

Remember that a little bit can go a long way. Frequently doing a few poses at a time may be better for you than practicing for two hours at a shot. You can do yoga any time of the day. When you practice in the morning, the body tends to be stiffer, but the mind is sharper. In an evening yoga session, the body is suppler, but the mind is duller.

THE UNION OF BODY AND BREATH

Yoga is very user friendly. It requires little in the way of equipment and space. The most important part is to show up, have an open mind, and be present with your self. Yoga is all about expanding self-awareness. Therefore, it is important to listen to your body and a trained practitioner as you practice postures and breathing techniques. It is imperative to safely practice in a nonaggressive manner. When opening up tight areas in the body that are unaccustomed to stretching, you may feel discomfort. This discomfort may be due to stiff joints, tight muscles, and/or tightness of *fascia* (the fibrous interconnective tissue that is like a web between skin and muscle and also encases organs). Discomfort could also be due to how your body is built: Some postures may not work for you the same way they work for another person. Every body is unique. So, it's important to go slowly and mindfully. Breathe into the postures during your entire practice: As you initiate a pose, build it, hold it, and release it; keep breathing, and notice how your body feels as you move and breathe.

Continuous breathing is the key. Often, shortness or holding of the breath is a good indication that you are working too hard or thinking too much. Let your breath inform and infuse your practice. Yoga is yoga because the breath is connected with the continuum of getting into the posture, being in the posture, and coming out of the posture. It is this connection of conscious movement with conscious breath that differentiates yoga poses from other physical disciplines, such as gymnastics or dance.

Yoga is an internally motivated practice. Comparing yourself to another practitioner or to a picture in a book and trying to mold your body into this ideal pose is not useful. All of us are different, and we come with bodies of all shapes and sizes and special needs. Some of us may be able to do backbends with ease and look beautiful doing them but struggle with forward bends. For others, the reverse may be true.

Yoga is not only about what you practice; it's about how you practice. Always modify poses as needed. This shows reverence for the body and compassion for ourselves and reflects the true meaning of yoga, a path of self-exploration where you learn to honor your experiences in the moment. You also develop trust in what you know deep inside as truth.

A quiet, well-ventilated, comfortably warm room keeps the muscles supple. If the room is too warm, it will be distracting, causing either irritation or lethargy (except in the types of yoga that are purposefully designated as hot yoga). A hardwood floor is terrific, but firm carpeting will also work fine. Clothing should be comfortable for full range of movement. T-shirts, leggings, and shorts are appropriate yoga gear. Yoga is done barefoot to tactilely feel, sense, and ground the feet.

PROPS

Some styles of yoga use a variety of props to help the body attain good alignment, balance, and ease in a pose. Props can enable you to perform a posture in proper alignment, thus allowing for a longer duration in the pose without strain and giving you the maximum benefit. The use of props helps to open the inner body while supporting muscular effort and minimizing strain and excessive striving in a pose. People with medical problems and the elderly will find the use of props invaluable in helping them practice poses that they might otherwise be unable to do.

There are many different props that can be used to enhance your practice. They can be purchased through catalogs and at some yoga centers and health food stores, such as Whole Foods. Here is a list of simple props, some of which may already be part of your household:

- **Sticky or nonslip mat:** This is a useful prop that provides traction and grip so you can concentrate on doing the posture without worrying about slipping.
- **Strap or belt:** A strap has many uses; for example, stretching the hamstrings in a variety of poses or making a "longer arm" for shoulder-opening exercises.
- **Three firm cotton or wool blankets:** Blankets are handy for sitting on and for placing under the knees, head, and torso for headstands and shoulderstands.
- **Metal or wooden chair without arms:** A chair is wonderful for supported and modified poses.
- **Wooden or foam block or a phone book:** This comes in handy in "bringing the floor to you" in many postures (for example, if you are in a standing forward bend and your hands don't reach the floor, a block placed under each hand eases the effort and stretch in the hamstrings); an old phone book can be encased in strong tape (duct tape works well).
- **Empty wall space:** A wall is a very useful tool to reinforce correct alignment, symmetry, and balance.

You Are Where You Are

Just as you should not be intimidated by yoga, neither should you be too eager to achieve the "perfect" pose and correct bad postural habits immediately. It took a lifetime to get you where you are today. One yoga class won't change all that. In yoga, being present to each moment along the journey is more important than the destination—and it's also a lot more interesting!

THE VALUE OF YOGA CLASSES

Attending yoga classes, with a teacher, can enhance your yoga practice. It is important for your understanding and growth for a teacher to observe you, someone who can provide feedback about your practice. Very often, we think we are doing correct action in our poses, but there are misalignments and unawareness that can detract from the precision and benefits of the pose. Having someone's eyes on you and his/her careful guidance can increase your awareness and stimulate your self-knowledge.

The teacher may challenge your way of being in a pose and suggest new actions that will enhance and deepen your practice. Subtleties you might never have thought of can become known to you. Then you can go back home, recharged and motivated, and practice with this new-found awareness.

The group energy of a class, plus being in community with like-minded individuals, can enhance your experience of yoga. You can share experiences with class members and help increase each other's awareness and knowledge.

UNITE BODY, MIND, AND SOUL

Remember that the goal is not the pose (known as asana) itself. Yoga is about the meditative process, from beginning to end, which includes reflecting on the effects of the poses. The asanas create different effects:

- Standing poses enhance vitality.
- Seated poses are calming.
- Twists are cleansing.
- Supine poses are restful.
- Prone poses are energizing.
- Inverted postures increase mental strength.
- Balancing poses create lightness and build focus.
- Backbends are exhilarating.
- Jumping develops agility.

Let's take a closer look at these beneficial effects and the 5-minute strategies we can use to enjoy them.

ENERGIZE YOURSELF

Yoga postures move the spine in these different ways:

- Forward
- Backward
- Side to side
- Twisting from one side to the other

Moving the spine in this way keeps the spine supple and healthy and nourishes the entire nervous system. The asanas release tension and blocked energy; lengthen and strengthen muscles; and tone, stimulate, and massage the internal organs. As a result, the muscles and organs are bathed in blood, nutrients, and *prana* (life force). Every cell is rejuvenated and cleansed. Respiration, cardiac function, circulation, nervous system function, elimination, and mental clarity improve. Fatigue and stress are reduced.

YOUR SPINE CHECKLIST

Yoga helps counteract the detrimental effects on the spine that result from the way we often sit, stand, and even sleep. During the course of most days, do you:

- Sit at a desk?
- Use a computer?
- Stand on your feet?
- Drive a vehicle?
- Lay on the couch?
- Sleep on a soft mattress?
- Carry a backpack or big purse?
- Wear high heels?

Doing any of these for a length of time can compromise the health of your back. Yoga can help you keep your spine supple and healthy.

TADASANA

Tadasana, the mountain pose, is the basic standing pose. Like a mountain, you want a broad, stable base from which to extend to the sky. Tadasana teaches you how to stand properly. You learn how to balance, center, ground, and extend.

Start by placing your feet together, joining the big toes and inner ankles if possible. Otherwise, stand so the ankles, knees, and hips are lined up, one over the other. When viewed from the side, the ear, shoulder, hip, knee, and ankle should form a straight, vertical line, with your arms by your sides (see Figure 6-1).

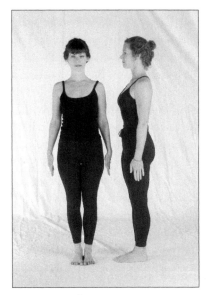

Figure 6-1: Tadasana

Create your yoga feet by spreading the toes, pressing into the big and little toe mounds and the center of the heel. Bring the weight a little more into the heels. Lift your arches as you ground the feet. Enhance this action by lengthening your leg muscles all the way up to your hips. Lift the top of the kneecaps by contracting the quadriceps muscle. Firm the muscles of the thigh to the bone.

Now you have created a strong and stable base from which the torso will be able to extend. This is like creating the mantle for the mountain to rise out of. Place your hands on your hips, and extend the sides of the body from your hips to your armpits. This action creates length and space in the spine.

Bring your arms back to your sides without losing the lift of the spine, and lengthen up through the crown of your head. Try to balance your head over the pelvis. Make sure the shoulders are relaxed and not riding up to the ears. Press your shoulder blades into your back. Lift the top of the chest and broaden the collarbones. Breathe fully, balancing ease with effort. Open the body to receive the breath, remaining aware of how it feels to be in alignment. Be the observer and the observed, the seer and the seen.

Tadasana can be done with the back to the wall for alignment. The tactile feedback from the back on the wall will aid in the sense of lengthening the torso. Tadasana can also be performed lying down, with the feet flush against the wall. This is an excellent way to feel the two-way action of the feet pressing, spreading, and lengthening in one direction, while the legs grow long in the opposite direction. The muscle action of the legs hugging the bone is also more pronounced when lying down because the floor provides feedback and there is no need to balance on the feet, as when standing. Tadasana is especially good for you because it:

- Teaches you how to stand correctly with proper alignment
- Develops agility

- Corrects minor misalignments of legs
- Strengthens ankles
- Relieves backache and neck strain
- Opens the chest

AGE YOURSELF GRACEFULLY

Several yoga postures are antiaging and antigravity—they reduce the sagging of organs and muscles due to aging and gravity's constant pull. The saying "You're as young as your spine" is absolutely true. Regular practice of yoga postures maintains the suppleness and youth of the spine. The postures also develop coordination and balance—essential for preventing falls. They improve posture and increase knowledge of body mechanics. Yoga also improves your circulation and can help deal with arthritis.

Play for Fitness Mindful Moment

Think back to your childhood—how flexible, playful, and in tune with your body you were. Remember that feeling—and notice when you feel it again, now.

As people grow older, as life slows down a bit, and as their responsibilities change, the desire to go inward and contemplate life grows. The system of yoga provides a wonderful framework for that inward search and growth. Conscious relaxation and meditation are time-tested tools for contemplation and inner wisdom.

YOU'RE AS YOUNG AS YOUR SPINE MINDFUL MOMENT

For the next twenty-four hours, observe how you carry yourself throughout the day—in the car, at your desk, when you walk down the street, etc. When do you slump? When do you stand up straight?

When you notice the slouching, can you mindfully change your position?

KEEP YOURSELF FIT

Yoga is a wonderful way to get into shape. The postures tone organs and develop long, lean muscles. The practice of forward bends, backbends, lateral poses, twists, and inversions balances and works every muscle, bone, joint, and organ in the body. Weight-bearing yoga poses, crucial for healthy bones, provide one of the best exercise systems known to humankind. Muscle flexibility and strength and joint range of motion greatly increase. Stamina and endurance also improve.

CIRCULATE YOURSELF

Yoga postures promote better blood and lymph circulation throughout the body. Let's take a look at the various kinds of postures and how each kind can improve circulation.

REVERSE GRAVITY WITH INVERSIONS

Inversions, such as the headstand and shoulderstand, reverse the flow of gravity, improving the blood supply to the lungs and brain and giving the legs and heart a rest. Pressure of the abdominal cavity against the diaphragm exercises the diaphragm and heart muscles. Inversions promote better sleep quality because they relax the sympathetic nervous system, enabling the relaxation response to kick in.

EASY INVERSION

Viparita Karani is the legs-up-the-wall pose. Place a bolster or one to three horizontally folded blankets against a wall. Lie on your side, with the left hip on the support, buttocks close to the wall, and the knees bent. Roll onto your back, and swing the legs up the wall. Rest the legs on the wall, the lower back and sacrum on the support, and the rest of the torso on the floor (see Figure 6-2). Outstretch the arms horizontally, with the palms facing up. The eyes may close and soften. Breathe naturally, and enjoy the relaxation and revitalization of the pose. To come out of the pose, bend the knees, and roll over onto your right side. Using your hands, press yourself up to a seated position.

Figure 6-2: Viparita Karani

You can also practice Viparita Karani with your legs wide apart. Or, you can bend your knees slightly if it is too intense a stretch for the hamstring muscles.

Inversions are not recommended during menstruation.

Note: People with hypertension, glaucoma, and cardiac disorders should practice this posture *only* under the guidance of a qualified yoga professional. It is not advised for people with detached retina and ear problems. Viparita Karani is especially good for you because it:

- Drains fluid from the legs
- Softens the belly and groins
- Reverses the effects of gravity
- Reverses the flow of blood and stimulates the lymphatic system
- Rests the heart and brain
- Relieves tired legs
- Revitalizes and relaxes

WRING IT OUT WITH TWISTS

Twists wring out the body like a wet towel, squeezing, massaging, and stimulating the organs and muscles; bringing in fresh blood and nutrients; and releasing toxins and wastes. They also reduce spinal, hip, and groin problems.

EASY TWIST

Jathara Parivartanasana is the belly-twisting pose (refer to Figure 6-3). Lie down, and bend the knees, with the feet flat on the floor. Inhale, lifting the feet away from the floor and bringing the knees to the chest. Extend the arms horizontally out to the sides on the floor. Stack the knees and ankles, and exhale as you let the knees come down to the right, toward the floor at a right angle. The legs will hover over the floor, with the lower leg holding up the upper leg. Gaze up at the ceiling. Feel the belly and the ribs spiral toward the left. Maintain the length of the spine on inhalation, twist on the exhalation, and roll the left shoulder down toward the floor (without forcing). Stay in the pose for several breaths, deepening the twist. Then inhale, bringing the knees back to center, and exhale as you go to the other side.

If hip mobility is restricted or the lower back is weak, place a folded blanket under the bottom leg for support.

Figure 6-3: Jathara Parivartanasana

Note: Jathara Parivartanasana is not recommended during menstruation, as there is too much activity in the abdominal area. It is also unsuitable for pregnant women. This pose works too strongly on the abdomen, and it is also a flat, horizontal position, which may put too much pressure on major arteries.

Jathara Parivartanasana is especially good for you because it:

- Provides a powerful, stimulating, and wringing action for the waist, abdomen, and lower back
- Strengthens transverse and oblique abdominal muscles
- Strengthens inner and outer thigh muscles

TWISTER MINDFUL MOMENT

The next time you feel overwhelmed by all the burdens of your life, do the belly-twisting pose. With each twist, picture yourself literally wringing out all of the unnecessary tasks and petty demands that weigh you down—and let them go.

FLUSH IT OUT WITH FORWARD BENDS

Forward bends rinse, squeeze, and flush the abdominal organs, encouraging proper digestion and elimination, and stretch and tone the organs in the back of the body. They quiet the mind and encourage introspection. The kidneys and adrenals are soothed by forward bends, relieving fatigue and renewing energy.

EASY FORWARD BEND

Uttanasana is a standing forward bend—an effective way to elongate the hamstring muscles and to lengthen and strengthen the back muscles and the spine. Stand in Tadasana. Inhale, root down onto the feet, stretch up through the legs, and elongate the spine as you contract the kneecaps and the quadriceps muscles to help the hamstrings lengthen. Firm the thigh muscles as you lift up through the crown of the head.

Roll the upper inner thighs and groin back, keeping the lower back broad. Draw the shoulder blades into the back to lift and open the chest. Maintain active yoga feet and a strong lift of the inner groin and legs. Actively lift and stretch your side ribs and spine up and over as you exhale and bend forward, folding at the hips.

Let the arms come down toward the floor. Place the fingertips on the floor in front of the feet (see Figure 6-4). The legs draw up so the spine can release down. Breathe, and allow the effects of gravity to release the back muscles, spine, and neck. Let your head relax. Contract the kneecaps and the quadriceps muscles to help the hamstrings lengthen. Broaden the backs of the calves and the backs of the thighs.

Figure 6-4: Uttanasana

When you are ready to come up, press the feet down, and keep the legs really active so that the strength of the thigh muscles supports the stretch of the hamstrings. This will prevent the feeling of locking the knees (hyperextension of the knees—pressing the knees back). Look forward, lengthening the crown of the head and the tailbone away from each other. Pull the abdomen in to protect the spine. Inhale, and come up with a concave back.

The knees can also be bent, allowing the spine to lengthen and the spinal muscles to strengthen.

Figure 6-5: Uttanasana, using blocks

You may want to widen the distance between the feet to hip-width or a little wider. Turn the toes in, and come into the pose. Turning the toes in deepens the hip crease, making it easier to bend from the hips and allowing the upper inner thighs and the groin to roll back, opening the lower back. When you reach for the ground, it will help to have blocks there to rest your hands on if you cannot comfortably and easily reach the floor.

Uttanasana is especially good for you because it:

- Reduces stomach discomfort
- Soothes the brain

- Intensely strengthens the back muscles and the hamstrings
- Relieves mental and physical exhaustion
- Slows down the heartbeat
- Tones the liver, spleen, and kidneys
- Decreases abdominal and back pains during menstruation

RAG DOLL MINDFUL MOMENT

The next time you're in a forward fold, hold each elbow with the opposite hand, and hang there for a moment like a rag doll, loose and long. As you hang there, release any stress you may feel with a big, loud sigh. Try this whenever you need to: literally and figuratively, hang loose.

OPEN YOUR HEART WITH BACKBENDS

Backbends squeeze the kidneys and adrenal glands and stretch and tone the organs in the front of the body. The lungs and heart are opened, bringing more breath and circulation throughout the body.

Note: The heart is exercised by the different postures, producing many benefits similar to aerobic exercise—with one important exception: Through yoga postures, the heart is not stressed as it is in aerobic activities, such as running or spinning. The heart receives the actions of the various postures through toning, stimulating, and massaging actions.

EASY BACKBEND

Setu Bandhasana is a bridge pose. Lie on your back, with the knees bent and feet flat on the floor, a little wider than hip-width apart. The arms are bent next to the waist, with the fingers stretching up to the ceiling. Palms face each other. Press the upper arms down for grounding to provide extension and length for the side ribs. Inhale, and press the feet down as you lift the hips slightly off the floor (see Figure 6-6). Do not tuck your pelvis or aggressively press the pelvis up, as this will compress and jam the lower back. Imagine that the shape of the pelvis resembles a hammock.

Figure 6-6: Setu Bandhasana preparation

As you press the feet down, try to drag your heels back to your shoulders without actually moving them. This action will contract your hamstrings, lengthen your quadriceps muscles, and keep the strain out of your lower back. Support the lifting of the hips with the hamstrings, and avoid overgripping of the buttocks. Broaden the chest. Breathe, and stay in the pose for several breaths. Exhale, release, and come down with a neutral spine. Relax, and then repeat the pose.

You can also try interlocking your fingers underneath you (see Figure 6-7). Roll onto the outer edges of the upper arm. Or, place a belt around the front of the ankles (see Figure 6-8). Hold on to each strap of the belt with your hands. To support your back, you can also place a vertical block underneath the sacrum (see Figure 6-9).

*Figure 6-7: Setu Bandhasana with interlocked
fingers*

Figure 6-8: Setu Bandhasana with belt around ankles

Figure 6-9: Setu Bandhasana with block under sacrum

Note: Don't practice Setu Bandhasana during menstruation or pregnancy. If you suffer from lower-back pain, avoid this pose.

Setu Bandhasana is especially good for you because it:

- Prepares you for shoulderstands and backbends
- Increases flexibility of the spine
- Stretches the front of the body, including the groin and thighs
- Lengthens the back of the neck
- Strengthens the back of the body
- Stimulates the thyroid and parathyroid glands

BUILD A BRIDGE MINDFUL MOMENT

Whenever you feel stuck in your life, come into bridge pose. Picture where you are now and where you want to be. Hold the pose, and build the bridge you need to get from here to there in your mind. This active visualization will help you cross every bridge in your life when you come to it with poise and confidence.

Yoga versus Walking

Yoga Journal reported a recent study in which a group of people who walked twenty minutes a day, three times a week were compared to a group of yoga practitioners who did standing poses twenty minutes a day, three times a week. Guess who received the greater cardiovascular benefit? The yogis did!

REV UP YOUR YIN SELF

Yoga is fabulous for women of all ages. Many of the poses are terrific for the health of the reproductive organs. It is therapeutic for menstrual, perimenopausal, and menopausal symptoms. A relaxing menstruation practice focuses on resting the abdominal area and emphasizes supported, seated forward bends; wide-legged poses; and basic supported backbends, which help lessen backache, cramping, fatigue, and excessive bleeding. Perimenopausal and menopausal women frequently experience mood swings, insomnia, fatigue, hot flashes, redistribution of body fat, and irregular bleeding. An appropriate yoga practice can alleviate many of these symptoms.

EASY PELVIS OPENER

Supta Baddha Konasana is the supported bound-angle pose. Stack one to three vertically folded blankets (one on top of the other) behind you, with the narrow end a few inches away from your buttocks. Sit cross-legged, spine straight. Bend the knees out to the sides, and join the soles of the feet together. Draw the heels in toward the pelvis at a comfortable distance for the knees and hips.

Place your hands on either side of the blankets, pull your belly button toward the spine for support, and lower your back (keeping it extended) and head onto the blankets. Let your arms come out to the sides, with the palms facing up. They will be off the blankets.

Close your eyes. Relax completely. This is a wonderful restorative posture. Stay in the pose for five to ten minutes, depending on your comfort level. Observe your breath and the expansion of the torso on inhalation and the contraction of the body on exhalation.

To come out of the pose, bring your knees together, and carefully roll off the blankets onto your right side. Press your hands down to bring yourself to a seated position.

It may be necessary to place a folded blanket under your head so your chin is neither pressing into your chest nor sticking way up in the air. Your chin can be level with your forehead or a little lower. You want to retain the natural (concave) curve of the neck. Your legs can be propped up with additional blankets or blocks for extra support (see Figure 6-10).

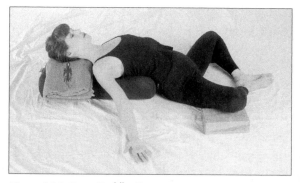

Figure 6-10: Supta Baddha Konasana

Some modifications:

For pregnant women, lying flat is not recommended. Instead, stack the blankets like stairs to allow the torso to lie on an incline.

If you have lower-back pain, come out of the pose, and readjust the height of the blankets. See if this helps. Placing support under the thighs may ease the back. If you have knee pain, place support under the knees. Adjust the distance of the heels from the groin, creating a wider angle with the knees. Or, put a block between the feet, which takes the action out of the knees and places it into the hips.

Note: If pain persists, do not stay in the pose.

Supta Baddha Konasana is especially good for you because it:

- Eases menstrual discomfort
- Opens the chest, abdomen, pelvis, inner thighs, and groin
- Deepens the breath
- Benefits the health of the ovaries and the prostate gland
- Regulates blood pressure
- Relieves varicose veins and sciatica
- Helps a prolapsed uterus
- Tones the kidneys

REV UP YOUR YANG SELF

In general, men have dense, bulky, tight muscles. Yoga postures can go a long way toward loosening and lengthening those knotty muscles. As men approach middle age, many experience prostate problems. Practicing a variety of postures, particularly forward bends and poses that open the pelvis and hips, is preventive health for the prostate gland and the lymph glands. (The lymphatic system, which circulates lymph fluid, picking up and eliminating waste throughout the body, greatly benefits from yoga postures and breathing exercises. The lymphatic system does not move on its own. It has to be pumped by the muscles.)

EASY PROSTATE POSE

Baddha Konasana is the bound-angle pose. Sit cross-legged, spine straight. Bend the knees out to the side, and join the soles of the feet. Press the soles of the feet together, pressurizing the balls of the feet and the heels, while you peel the toes away from each other. Observe what this feels like. What actions do you observe in the legs? Check in with your breath. Using the hands, draw the feet in toward the pelvis to where it is comfortable. Let the thighs release down to the floor. Open the soles of the feet with your hands, as if they were the pages of an open book. Inhale, and press into the buttock bones (see Figure 6-11). Elongate the spine all the way to the crown of the head. Exhale fully, and lift the top chest, keeping the shoulder blades on the back. Remain for several breaths. Join the knees together, then sit cross-legged, spine straight. You may want to sit with the back against the wall for support.

Figure 6-11: Baddha Konasana

You can also try this pose sitting on a blanket to maintain an upright, level pelvis. Place the rounded corner of the folded blanket facing forward. Sit down, with the rounded corner under the pubis. This will allow the thighs and groin to release farther down to the floor. Or, place a rolled up blanket or a block under each knee for support and relaxation of the thigh muscles (see Figure 6-12).

Figure 6-12: Baddha Konasana with blocks

Bring the feet farther forward into what is known as star pose. This will enable the knees and thighs to release farther to the floor. Fold forward from the hips no more than 45 degrees, maintaining a long spine and keeping the buttock bones planted on the floor (see Figure 6-13).

Figure 6-13: Star pose

You can also try placing the hands behind you, fingertips on the floor, as you come forward (see Figure 6-14). This is a great way to learn how to bend forward from the hips without the shoulders and upper back rounding.

Figure 6-14: Baddha Konasana with fingertips behind hips

Note: If you suffer from knee pain and none of the modifications help, refrain from doing the pose.

Baddha Konasana is especially good for you because it:

- Stretches the inner thighs and groin
- Opens the pelvis and lower back
- Reduces sciatic pain
- Maintains the health of the kidneys, prostate, ovaries, and bladder
- Is a wonderful pose for pregnancy, helping with delivery and diminishing varicose veins
- Eases menstrual discomfort
- Is recommended for deep breathing and meditation practices

OPEN TO YOUR MASCULINE ENERGY MINDFUL MOMENT

Whenever you feel like you need to reconnect with your masculine side, do Baddha Konasana. Breathe in yang energy—fiery and forceful. Imagine yourself as the sun, pulsating with the heat that powers the planet. Breathe out excess lethargy and passivity. Repeat.

RELIEVE YOUR CHRONIC AILMENTS

Common chronic ailments, such as arthritis, osteoporosis, obesity, asthma, heart disease, addictions (many twelve-step programs have incorporated yoga into their programs with good results), back problems, knee injuries, arthritis, carpal tunnel syndrome, mild depression, sinus problems, and headaches (to name just a few!), can be relieved through regular yoga practice.

Yoga for cancer patients emphasizes stress management utilizing awareness, centering, and breathing techniques; gentle movement; deep relaxation; and meditation. Yoga is being used as a successful healing modality in conjunction with other therapies at highly respected cancer retreats, such as Commonweal in Bolinas, California, and Smith Farm in Hallowood, Maryland. These yoga techniques help cancer patients cope with the stress of the disease and with the effects of their treatment, such as fatigue, nausea, flulike symptoms, and chemotherapy-induced menopause.

People with multiple sclerosis have found yoga to be extremely beneficial in maintaining muscle, tone, strength, and flexibility. Yoga also helps restore a sense of control over their lives and enhances their overall quality of life. Note: If you suffer from any of these ailments, be sure to check with your physician before taking up yoga—and do learn the poses under the guidance of an experienced and certified yoga instructor.

RELAX YOURSELF

Yoga's unique combination of postures and deep breathing invigorates the entire body–mind system. These specific yogic breathing techniques are called *pranayama*, which controls the breath and, ultimately, the mind. The practice of pranayama boasts many curative benefits, as it helps to:

- Calm and strengthen the respiratory and nervous systems
- Balance and replenish the body's vital energy
- Lessen fatigue
- Quiet the mind and calm the emotions

Conscious relaxation techniques systematically guide you into a state of deep relaxation. As the noisy chatter of your mind recedes, your body is able to let go and release muscular tension. As your body lets go, the breath rate slows and deepens so the respiratory system is allowed to rest. Slow, deep breathing encourages relaxation and calmness just as a quick, shallow breath invites anxiety and action.

As the breath rate slows down, the heartbeat responds and also becomes slower. This positively affects the entire circulatory system and rests the heart, allowing it to rejuvenate. The sympathetic nervous system, always ready to gear up for action, gets the message that it is okay to relax, and then the parasympathetic nervous system initiates the relaxation response.

The endocrine glands, responsible for much of your emotional and physical well-being, receive the message to relax. (In this stress-driven society, the adrenal glands in particular become overused and depleted.)

This deep relaxation goes to the very core of decreasing fatigue and unraveling you from the inside out like a knotted ball of twine. You emerge from this experience full of energy, as if you've just returned from a mini-vacation from your stressful life.

EASY BREATHING EXERCISE

Sit cross-legged (which is known as *Sukhasana* in Sanskrit) on two folded blankets (refer to Figure 6-15). Cup the fingertips, place them on the floor by the hips, and lightly lift the buttocks and stretch the torso up to lengthen the spine and make space in the body for the breath to come in. Lower the buttocks back down to the floor while maintaining the length of the sides of the body.

Figure 6-15: Sukhasana on a blanket

Bend the elbows, and place the back of the hands on top of the thighs, close to the hips. Press the buttock bones down as you lift and broaden the collarbones and stretch the sternum up. Draw the upper arms back slightly to bring the shoulder blades down and into the back. Bring the upper back in without jutting out the front ribs.

Inhale the breath, and lengthen up through the back of the neck and the head. Exhale, and bring the chin to the chest by bending the neck forward at the seventh cervical vertebra. (This is where the neck meets the shoulders). Close and soften the eyes. The chest remains lifted throughout the exercise.

Observe your breathing pattern: the length of the inhalation, exhalation, and pauses in between. Be aware of the movement of the rib cage, expanding with inhalation and contracting on exhalation. With each inhalation, feel the rise and fall of the chest. The breath will fill the chest more than the abdomen. Make sure the chest doesn't collapse when you exhale the breath. Stay in this position for five minutes.

You can also try this type of pranayama while sitting with your back against the wall for support. Or, try sitting upright in a chair, without leaning against the chair back. Place the hands on top of the thighs.

Pranayama in Sukhasana is especially good for you because it teaches you how to sit for meditation and trains you to observe the breath.

FULFILL YOURSELF

Meditation, a part of yoga, is a powerful tool for reducing tension and stress and for bringing you back in touch with your true self and your inner reality. In meditation, you sit and watch the workings of the mind as an impassionate observer. Through meditation you observe the fluctuations of the mind and realize the preciousness of the present moment. The events of the past and the future loosen their grip on you, and everyday concerns take a backseat as you focus on yourself. The frenetic pace of life slows down and becomes manageable, even peaceful. What seemed so earth-shattering just minutes ago is now put into perspective. You become aware of thought patterns and the vacillation of emotions.

EASY MANTRA MEDITATION

In mantra meditation, you simply repeat a word or phrase to clear your mind. Select a word or short phrase with personal meaning to you, one that is inspiring. Or, simply choose *Om*, the mantra most commonly associated with yoga.

Sit or rest comfortably, close your eyes, repeat the word or phrase, and focus on it so that all your other worries disappear. Over time, you may repeat the mantra less as your concentration improves.

BOOST YOUR SELF-ESTEEM AND BODY IMAGE

Yoga helps develop positive self-esteem and a positive body image and a more comfortable and realistic view of yourself. This is sorely needed in a world in which we are incessantly bombarded by media images of thin, beautiful, airbrushed models and celebrities (truly the impossible dream for most of us).

The practice of yoga creates physical, mental, and emotional confidence and stability. The body becomes stronger and more agile. The mind begins to listen to the needs of the body and cultivates a mind–body relationship. Self-esteem and confidence grow. The inner voice is awakened. Understanding of your emotions deepens. The need to stuff emotions out of consciousness through overeating or to be in control by starving the body diminishes. As you listen internally, you begin responding to appropriate internal cues and eating nutritious foods when you're hungry, contributing positively to your overall health.

YOGA DIET MINDFUL MOMENT

Yoga will help you lose weight but probably not in the way you'd expect. It's not only the physical exertion in the poses that helps you lose weight. Just as significant is the attitude you develop from the practice of yoga. You learn to listen to your body—and give it what it really needs. To help bring your eating habits into conscious awareness, ask yourself:

- Am I hungry now?
- Am I eating just because it's time to eat a meal?
- Am I enjoying this meal?
- Am I eating in front of the television or reading something instead of focusing solely on my meal?
- Am I responding to other people's needs or giving into societal pressures by eating these foods or eating at this time?
- What emotions do I associate with this food choice?
- Am I eating out of frustration or tension, and if so, what do I eat when I feel this way?
- When I feel relaxed, what do I feel like eating?
- Is there another activity besides eating that I could do to satisfy my needs at this time?

Remember that conscious eating is a way of developing greater sensitivity to your needs. It reflects how you are in relationship to yourself. Can you translate the caring and compassion that you show others to yourself?

THE PRINCIPLES OF CONSCIOUS EATING

- Eat in moderation.
- Eat only when hungry.
- Eat in a relaxed and quiet environment.
- Drink liquids that are warm or room temperature.
- Keep a variety of nutritious, wholesome foods in the house, such as fresh fruits, vegetables, and whole grains.
- Do not eat processed snack foods.
- Eat fewer sugary and salty foods.
- Make dietary changes gradually.

STRETCH YOURSELF

Yoga improves your posture in daily life. Frequently, yoga students comment that, as a result of doing yoga, they become increasingly aware of their posture and correct it during daily activities outside of class. Better physical alignment and posture are visually appealing and also say a lot about a person, but the effects go much deeper.

A person with rounded shoulders will have trouble breathing fully because the chest is collapsed. This is also the posture of a depressed, overwhelmed person, who may have neck discomfort because the neck's natural curve has changed as a result of poor postural habits. Someone with a *sway back* (an exaggerated lower-back curve) may experience low-back pain as a result of a forward-tilting pelvis and shortened, tight lower-back muscles and may possibly suffer from compression in the lower back.

When the body is in good alignment, the bones stack up properly, from the feet up. If the *femur* (thigh) bones insert properly into the pelvis, the hips will be level with each other and create a balanced sacrum, crucial to the alignment and health of the spine. The *sacrum* is the fulcrum upon which the spine rests.

Many people experience chronic back pain as a result of sacrum dysfunction. A balanced spine arising out of the pelvis will ensure that the torso is well supported and free to bend in all directions. When the bones insert properly into the joints, the muscles can fall into place and work in a balanced, coordinated manner, and the organs will have enough space to function optimally.

A physically aligned body promotes mental, emotional, and spiritual alignment and clarity. For example, how many times have you had a headache, neck ache, or backache and found it impossible to concentrate or think? Didn't you become irritable and short tempered? Yoga helps prevent that.

EASY BACK RELIEF

Balasana is the child's pose. Start on the hands and knees, with the hands under the shoulders and the knees under the hips. Inhale, and, on the exhalation, draw your buttocks back to rest on your heels. Press the hands on the floor, extending into the fingertips and stretching back through the sides of the body to the hips (see Figure 6-16). Let the forehead rest on the floor. While in the pose, inhale, and feel the expansion of the waist and lower back. Exhale, and observe the contraction of the ribs and lungs and the softening of the body as the breath leaves the body. Stay for several breaths, and then come back up and release the pose.

For enhanced lengthening of the spine, practice Balasana by walking the hands to the right for several breaths and then to the left. This stretch isolates the action on one side of the body at a time.

Figure 6-16: Balasana

STRENGTHEN YOURSELF

Professor Steven A. Hawkins and faculty yoga teacher Bee Beckman, of the Department of Kinesiology and Physical Education at California State University, recently conducted a study that included eighteen women, from 18 to 65 years of age, who had no former yoga experience. Half of the group participated in two yoga classes a week and also practiced by themselves three times a week. Some of the required poses practiced were triangle, half moon, extended side angle, and warriors I and II. The women in the control group had to continue their normal level of activity throughout the study.

Third Eye Mindful Moment

In Balasana, you lay your forehead on the mat, stimulating the third eye. The third eye is the center of intuition, vision, and clairvoyance. What vision would you like to manifest for yourself? Visualize this dream in detail. Breathe it in—and breathe out any obstacles in your way.

Bone density scans were done at the beginning of the study and then six months later. In the yoga group, the bone density scans done after six months showed that the bone density of the spine had significantly increased, while those in the control group had no change in their bone density levels. More studies with larger population groups are needed to get a clearer picture, but it is evident that weight-bearing yoga postures (arm balances, inversions, and standing poses) maintain bone density, increase bone density, and help prevent osteoporosis and fragile bones.

Not surprising, stress adversely affects bone density. Overdoing aerobic activity leads to decreased body fat and increases the likelihood of osteoporosis. Living a stressful lifestyle full of adrenaline rushes depletes calcium and imbalances hormonal activity. A consistent yoga practice, which includes weight-bearing and restorative postures, relaxation, and meditation, helps lessen the effects of stress and restores balance.

ADHO MUKHA SVANASANA

Adho Mukha Svanasana is the downward-facing dog pose. If you've ever seen a dog stretching, you know that this pose looks like an upside-down *V*. It is beautiful to watch. The dog grounds into its four paws and then lengthens up the front legs and back legs, through the spine to the buttocks. It looks so easy and natural, and it is a terrific stretch! Downward-facing dog is one of the most frequently practiced yoga poses.

Start on the hands and knees. Place the hands under the shoulders and the knees directly under the hips. The inner arms face each other, and the elbows are straight and firm (see Figure 6-17). Let the shoulder blades come onto the back. Observe that the upper arm bones connect into the shoulder socket. The pelvis is in a neutral position, horizontal to the floor. Tuck the toes under.

Figure 6-17: Adho Mukha Svanasana, from all fours

Plant the hands firmly on the floor, and evenly spread the fingers apart. Press the palms, knuckles, and fingers into the floor. Especially, press down the pointer-finger knuckle, and balance the weight on either side of the hand (just like you do for the feet in standing poses). These are important actions to maintain throughout the pose because the hands are part of the pose's foundation and they must stay rooted for extension of the spine to occur.

Inhale the breath; evenly lift the hips, with bent knees, and press the hands and toes down (Figure 6-18). On the exhalation, straighten the legs, and let the head drop between the arms. Relax the neck. Press the front of the thighs back to elongate the torso. Press the hands down, extending into the fingertips. Then stretch the arms away from the hand, all the way up to the buttock bones (see Figure 6-19). Let the spine lengthen, from the top of the head to the tailbone, into one long line of extension.

Figure 6-18: Adho Mukha Svanasana

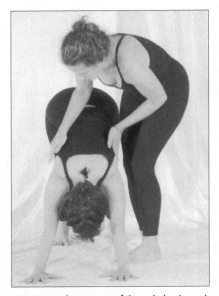

Figure 6-19: Lengthening up of the side body and spine

Lift the heels up, resisting the shoulders moving forward, and continue stretching all the way up the back of the legs to the buttock bones. Now, lengthen the heels down, but keep stretching the back of the legs up. Lift the kneecaps and firm the thighs. The heels are stretching toward the floor. They might even make it to the floor, but do not force this action if it is not happening. Lift the shins out of the top of the ankles as you press the heels down. The toes are also working, spreading, grounding, with arches of the feet lifting to enhance the upward extension of the legs. Fully stretch the legs. Keep the arms as long as possible. Bending the elbows will make it difficult to transfer the weight of the body from the arms to the legs. Remain in the pose for several breaths, extending the spine on the inhalation. Then bend the knees and come down.

You can put the back of the heels against the wall for extra grounding. Or, try placing the hands and feet wider apart than shoulder-width. This helps ease tight shoulders and hips and is a good way to start practicing downward dog. If the hamstrings are tight, keep the knees slightly bent and focus on lengthening the spine and drawing the tailbone up and back. As time goes on and the hamstrings loosen, fully stretch the legs.

For a more challenging way to come into downward dog, lie on your belly, with your hands on the floor under the shoulders and fingers facing forward. Extend the legs behind you, and tuck the toes way under. Inhale the breath; press the hands and the toes down; and stretch the arms up, lifting the body off the floor. The body is compact. No sagging of the abdomen, hips, and thighs. Lift the hips and buttocks up, bend the hips, and press the legs back into downward dog.

If you have wrist problems, you can put a rolled-up washcloth under the palms to bring the weight into the knuckles and fingers and take pressure off the wrists. Practice with awareness, gradually building up strength in the hands and wrists.

If you have shoulder pain, pay particular attention to how weight is distributed through the hands, arms, and shoulders and transferred up the spine to the tailbone. Of course, if there is pain, come down from the pose. Adho Mukha Svanasana is especially good for you because it:

- Stretches hamstring and calf muscles
- Lengthens the spine
- Strengthens the upper body, arms, and wrists
- Increases bone density as a weight-bearing exercise
- Increases shoulder flexibility
- Opens the chest
- Rests the heart and quiets the brain, as a mild inversion

Downward-facing dog is a pose that builds strength and perseverance. When you need to call on those qualities of doggedness, do this pose. Meditate on the weight you need to carry—and what you don't.

BALANCE YOURSELF

Yoga has a profound impact on the emotions. Forward bends are introverted postures and, thus, have a quieting effect, reducing agitation and anxiety. Backbends are extroverted postures that exhilarate and help to open the body and release held emotions, such as sadness and grief. Inversions turn your world upside down, literally, and allow you to change your perspective on life—they are mood elevators. Twists are cleansing. Specific breathing exercises can be done to calm or energize the individual. Relaxation and meditation practices are also extremely useful, depending on the situation.

Of course, yoga is *not* a substitute for mental therapy. Mental health professionals should be utilized when necessary. The combination of yoga and psychotherapy can be a very powerful accelerator to personal healing and growth, as the mind and body are jointly explored and united.

EASY BALANCE POSE

Vrksasana, the tree pose, develops balance, focus, and upward stretch, much like a tree, which has a strong, extensive root system, allowing it to grow tall and branch out.

Start by standing in Tadasana. Gaze straight ahead, with a soft but focused gaze. Shift your weight to the left leg, root down into the balls of the feet and heels, and press firmly down with the big toe and the little toe. Turn your right foot out to the side. Then, bring your right foot up to the inside of the left leg to where it is comfortable. You may use your hand to help bring the foot up the leg. Press the sole of the right foot against the inside of the left leg, leg against foot, as if they were pressing the spine up. If the foot does not easily stay on the leg, it is fine to leave it on the floor, heel turned in, resting against the inner heel or ankle of the left foot. Maintain the grounding in the left foot and the extension in the left leg, taking care not to hyperextend the leg. Press the big toe down, and lift the kneecap. Extend the arms out to the sides, with the palms facing up. Stretch all the way from the centerline in the body to the fingertips. On an inhalation, take the arms up over the head, stretching from the side ribs to the fingertips, palms facing each other (see Figure 6-20).

Continue breathing through the nostrils, relaxing the throat and diaphragm and softening the front ribs and belly. Balance ease with effort. Stay in Vrksasana for several breaths or as long as you feel comfortable and can maintain the pose. To come out of the pose, exhale, and release the arms to the side as the right leg comes back into Tadasana. Repeat on the other side.

You can also practice Vrksasana with your arms wider apart, in the shape of a *V*, to maintain stretch and extension in the arms and straight elbows with which to lift the ribs and torso up off the hips. Or, you can do the tree pose with your back against the wall for support and balance. You can also turn sideways and place a hand on the wall to maintain balance.

Figure 6-20: Vrksasana

Vrksasana is especially good for you because it:

- Tones and strengthens leg muscles
- Strengthens the ankles
- Improves balance, focus, and coordination
- Opens the hips
- Lengthens the spine
- Expands the chest for fuller breathing

REV UP YOUR SEX LIFE

The physical yoga postures stimulate and strengthen the body and improve circulation. The pelvic organs and the muscles supporting them, particularly the perineal muscles (located between the anus and the genitals), and the pelvic floor are toned, oxygenated, and flushed with fresh blood and nutrients. This can contribute to greater sensitivity and responsiveness during intercourse.

Tight areas, such as shoulders, hips, hamstrings, groin, and lower back, loosen and become more flexible. Greater flexibility allows for a greater variety of sexual positions and ease of movement.

Body image and self-esteem frequently improve as a result of doing yoga, and this can only enhance and improve your sex life. Often, people are inhibited and self-conscious of how their bodies look and how their partners might react. People tend to think that their physical appearance and performance are being judged during sex. This attitude can be a total turnoff for both you and your partner because it does not allow you to be playful and focus on the fun you might have together if you weren't so concerned with your external appearance. Being comfortable in your own skin makes a big difference in how you interact on an intimate level — and yoga can help.

Get It On Mindful Moment

Couples yoga is a playful way to enjoy practicing yoga. Most partner poses involve mirroring the pose to each other (for example, doing tree pose with the straight-legged side of the body in contact with your partner's side). The communication and feedback between partners provides a unique opportunity to deepen intimacy.

The physical postures, breathing exercises, deep relaxation, and meditation help decrease fatigue and stress and promote relaxation. Less stress and fatigue translate into less irritability, more patience, and greater energy and emotional availability. A greater ability to relax helps to decrease inhibitions and increase sexual spontaneity and fun in bed.

Yoga focuses the mind. A wandering mind during sex does not allow you to be fully present and intimate with your partner. It might make for a great fantasy life but not for loving the one you're with!

CONTRAINDICATIONS

Many poses and breathing techniques in yoga are therapeutic. That said, you should avoid some actions if you suffer from certain conditions. Some contraindications include:

- **Cardiac disorders:** Do not put your arms over your head.
- **Menstruation:** Do not perform inversions.
- **Pregnancy:** Do not practice breath retention.
- **Glaucoma or eye problems, ear pain, or congestion:** Don't practice breath retention or inversions.
- **Hypertension:** Do not practice breath retention or inverted poses except for the legs-up-the-wall pose.

Before beginning any new physical practice (including yoga and breathing exercises), be sure to check with your physician. And, during a yoga class, any questions or concerns should be brought to the attention of your qualified yoga teacher for clarification. If anything feels out of sorts, if you start to feel lightheaded or dizzy, or if you feel sharp pain during a yoga class, come out of the pose and relax. If the symptom doesn't subside when you release the pose and rest for a moment, let the instructor know.

CHAPTER 7

STRETCH, BREATHE, RELAX!

"If you achieve one pose, that is enough."

— PATANJALI

As we have just seen, the benefits of yoga are many. The style of yoga you choose depends on you and your body and the particular benefits you're likely to enjoy:

If you're inflexible, with tight hamstrings and a tight lower back, you may want to create more flexibility and space within your body, your primary goal being to increase physical comfort and range of motion.

If you're extremely stressed out, suffering symptoms such as headaches and lower-back tightness, you may want to focus on relaxation, breathing, and meditation techniques as a way to manage stress and tension.

If you are recovering from illness or surgery, you may be interested in passive yoga postures.

If you're very athletic, you may want to be very active and challenged, sweating, building strength, and developing a leaner body.

The best way to explore all of the various styles of yoga is to sample several different classes until you find one that satisfies your needs. Classes vary widely in terms of asanas, pranayama, athleticism, relaxation, and more.

What do you want to get out of the experience? The teacher is an important factor in your decision. Ask the teacher for his/her credentials and background. The match between student and teacher is crucial. After attending a class, ask yourself:

- Did I receive attentive guidance from the teacher, or did I have to look around the class and imitate the other students?
- Do I feel a little sore from using my body differently, or did I actually get injured in class?
- Am I feeling energized and calm, or do I feel frustrated and stressed out?
- Was the class small enough for me to get the amount of individualized attention I want?
- Did I feel comfortable and at ease?
- Were the teacher's instructions clear enough that I could follow and learn from them?

SO MANY ASANAS, SO LITTLE TIME

Asanas are a vital part of yoga. The postures are more than physical exercises. They clean, control, and discipline the mind and body; sharpen the natural intelligence; and awaken every cell in the body. There are literally hundreds of yoga poses; the many different types of asanas help tone, balance, and stimulate every part of the body.

You'll learn more of these asanas as you continue your practice, along with how to put them together in sequences for best effect. (This is why it's good to try out lots of yoga teachers and classes, which will expose you to different asanas and different sequences.)

DEEPEN YOURSELF — WITH BODY AND BREATH

The breath is the vehicle for *prana*, the vital life force. It is the universal energy that sustains all life. The prana enters the body upon inhalation, supplying every cell with energy, oxygen, and nutrients. With exhalation, waste and toxins are released. The breath is the bridge between the physical and spiritual worlds.

THE ANATOMY OF THE BREATH

The lungs are not made of muscle tissue, but they have elasticity and can receive the actions of surrounding muscles. The lungs must depend on muscular action for their expansion and contraction.

It is the diaphragm, the *intercostals* (the muscles located between the ribs), and the abdominal muscles that play a key role in breathing. The diaphragm, located in the chest, is a large umbrella-shaped muscle responsible for 75 percent of the work. It attaches to the top of the *sternum* (the breastbone); the middle and lower ribs; and to the first, second, third, and fourth lumbar vertebrae in the lower spine (inserting on the back of the body). Under the diaphragm lies the abdominal organs and above it the heart and lungs.

With inhalation, the diaphragm comes down toward the abdomen and expands, making room for the incoming breath. Upon exhalation, the diaphragm rises up to release the air. As the lungs expand with the inhalation, the abdomen expands, the intercostal muscles lengthen and spread laterally, and the top chest (near the collarbones) expands and broadens.

This entire process is reversed during exhalation. The breath is squeezed out of the belly, the ribs and intercostal muscles contract, and the breath is pushed out of the body.

BREATHE LIKE A YOGI

When you begin practicing yoga, your respiration may be shallow, with small, fairly rapid breaths. The average person breathes sixteen to eighteen breaths per minute. As you continue your yoga practice, your rate of breath will become slower, and each inhalation and exhalation will become longer and fuller. Deeper breaths allow the energy to reach every cell.

The yoga postures open the body to receive the breath, resulting in increased elasticity of the lungs and intercostal muscles. Forward bends stretch the back of the body and fill the back of the lungs, backbends open the front of the body and the front of the lungs, and lateral bends lengthen the sides of the body and the space between the lungs (the intercostal muscles). Inversions bring greater oxygen and blood flow to the brain.

In yoga, the body is considered to be a container for the life force. The nervous system is the electrical circuitry, which conducts the energy of the body. The spinal column houses the central energy channel, called *sushumna*, and is the central energetic pathway. Two other main pathways are the *pingala*, to the right of the sushumna, and the *ida*, on the left side. Balance between the ida and pingala increases the energy flow to the sushumna. The ida channel cools the body and corresponds to the parasympathetic nervous system, while the pingala heats up the body and corresponds to the sympathetic nervous system. These main channels correspond to the central nervous system and are called *nadis*. There are thousands of smaller nadis comprising the peripheral nervous system. When awakened through meditation, *kundalini* (serpent power) energy rises up the spine (the sushumna), opening the various energy centers in the body and causing spiritual evolution within the individual.

Yogic breathing is almost always done through the nostrils. The nose is a complex and extremely efficient filtering system for foreign particles. As the breath enters the nostrils, it is moistened and warmed to body temperature. Breathing through the nose allows for deeper, fuller, and more controllable breathing.

Mouth breathing is for those times of athletic competition, such as sprint running, when the body is in oxygen deprivation due to the excessive demands being placed on it. Then, mouth breathing becomes the last resort. For these reasons, it is considered a waste of energy to breathe through the mouth.

THE COMPLETE BREATH EXERCISE

Lie down, with knees bent and feet on the floor, and begin breathing through your nostrils and observing your breath. Become aware of the natural length of your inhalation and exhalation and the pauses in between. Remain relaxed, without changing or forcing the breath. Let the breath flow smoothly and evenly. Relax your facial muscles and jaw.

Now, place your hands on your lower abdomen, allowing them to rest there lightly. As you breathe in, feel your hands fill with your breath as your belly gently expands. Upon exhalation, notice how your belly contracts, moving away from your hands and receding into your body. Spend ten to twelve breaths observing the movement of the breath in your belly.

Next, lightly place your palms on your lower front floating ribs. Let your wrists relax down to your body. Again, let the breath come into your hands upon inhalation, and feel your ribs contracting on exhalation. Do this for another ten to twelve breaths.

Last, place your hands on the collarbones, and on the inhalation, observe the breath filling the area under your hands. Notice how your top chest recedes with the exhalation. Practice this for ten to twelve breaths.

Then allow your arms to come back to your sides, palms facing up. Continue to watch your breath, feeling the three-part breathing pattern. You may find that the breath comes in more easily to one area than it does to another. For example, initially, on inhalation, many people find it difficult to fill the top chest. Over time and with practice, you will be able to breathe more fully and deeply, filling your entire body with the breath.

RAISING THE ARMS WITH THE BREATH EXERCISE

Stand with your feet directly under your hips. Plant your feet firmly on the floor, and lengthen up through your legs and your spine to the top of your head. Have your arms at your sides, palms facing forward. Begin normal, relaxed breathing through the nostrils.

As you inhale, raise your arms slowly, feeling your belly fill up, then feeling your ribs expand and the top of your chest broaden with the breath. Let your expanding belly, chest, and ribs help you to reach your arms up. At the top of the inhalation, the arms will be over your head. When exhalation naturally starts, press your palms down as you watch the breath leave the top chest and squeeze out of the lungs and the belly.

Allow the pressing down of your palms to help push the breath out of your body. Practice coordinating the lifting and lowering of the arms with the flow of the breath.

Do at least five breaths this way. Be aware of how you feel after this experience. Do you feel more grounded and internally connected? Are you calmer and more focused?

This breathing exercise is a wonderful way to learn about your breath and is also excellent for opening and warming up the body. Don't worry if your inhalation is finished before the breath reaches the top chest. With practice, your exhalation will become longer, and this will positively affect the length of the inhalation.

STRENGTHENING THE DIAPHRAGM EXERCISE

The diaphragm is a large and powerful muscle involved in the respiration process. Like any muscle, it needs to be exercised for it to become strong and function optimally.

Lie on your back, and place a 10-pound sandbag (or a bag of rice or flour) on your abdomen, just below the floating ribs. Then lie back and breathe normally, without force or strain, for five minutes. Don't try to lift the sandbag. Let the breath touch the sandbag. If you feel fatigued before five minutes have passed, lessen the duration of the exercise.

You will feel the weight of the sandbag as your chest rises and falls, but do not consciously try to lift the bag. Let your breath and the sandbag exercise your diaphragm muscle. A strong, not tense, diaphragm muscle will lead to fuller, deeper, and more efficient breathing and will also aid in the pumping and circulating of the lymphatic system.

After five minutes, take the sandbag off the diaphragm, and continue to observe your breath. You may notice a difference. Practice sandbag breathing for five minutes a day, gradually building up to ten minutes. Do this for a month, scheduling yourself for three days of practice and then one day off. Observe the changes in your breath. Your breathing will deepen and become more efficient, and the diaphragm will be stronger. This exercise can be repeated anytime to exercise and strengthen the diaphragm.

COORDINATING BREATH WITH MOVEMENT EXERCISE

Coordinate the breath with your movement. This is how to harness the vital energy necessary to move through the pose with ease.

In general, the inhalation is done while creating extension and expansion in the body. This is the preparation for the pose. Most movement into a pose is performed upon exhalation. An elongation of the front of the body will encourage inhalation, while a curling and shortening of the front body will invite exhalation. The exhalation also contracts the abdominals, which provide support and stability for the lower back. Coming down into a pose is done on the exhalation, and coming up out of a pose is done on the inhalation. Continuous breathing is vital regardless of the synchronization with the movement.

5-MINUTE BREATH CHECK-IN

Observe your breath during the day. Check in with your breath every hour at a specified time. Slow down, and tune in to the quality and length of the inhalation, exhalation, and the pauses in between. Notice if the breath is smooth or ragged, shallow or deep.

Take several breaths through your nostrils and then through your mouth, observing the differences. Was the length of the inhalation and exhalation the same? Does your mouth feel dry as a result of breathing through the mouth? Which style feels more comfortable? Initially, breathing through the nostrils may be difficult. But, soon, nose breathing will become more comfortable and natural.

ALL ROADS LEAD TO MINDFULNESS

Yoga is a time-honored way to rejuvenate your body, but there are many other ways you can experience mindfulness. Some people may experience it when running; hence, the runner's high. Others may experience mindfulness hoofing it on the hiking trail, rowing on the water, surfing the waves, biking the roads, swimming the seas, throwing hoops, swinging clubs, pulling weeds, or pounding the heavy bag. Be sure to explore any and all avenues for refreshing and renewing your body, on your own or with like-minded souls.

Just remember that in a pinch, mindfulness is as close as your yoga mat.

MINDFUL BODY, MINDFUL TEMPLE

Namaste. Your divine self has learned to quiet your mind and listen to your body. Now it's time to learn to commune with the divine because mindfulness is ultimately a journey of the soul.

Name Your Peace Mindful Moment

Make a list of words that resonate "peace" to you—people, places, things. Use these words as your mantra either alone or in combination.

"Yoga gave me the ability to calm down."

—CHRISTY TURLINGTON

CHAPTER 8

SAY A LITTLE MINDFUL PRAYER

"You don't have a soul. You are a Soul. You have a body."

—C. S. Lewis

Even as we quiet the mind and listen to the body, communing with the divine may seem improbable at best and impossible at worst. For many of us, our daily lives are too busy, too messy, too full of mundane details to encourage connecting with spirit.

And, yet, as they say, God is in the details. Learning to live a mindful life—day by day, hour by hour, minute by minute—can help you rediscover the sacred, however you may define it and however far removed from it you may feel now.

A SATORI A DAY

Even the craziest of days offers us opportunities to experience those aha! moments of clarity that illuminate our lives—and change us forever. Whether you see these soulful moments as whispers from God, blessings from the universe, or simply gifts from your subconscious doesn't really matter. What matters is that they happen, and with a little mindfulness, we can experience them more often.

You have most likely experienced these flashes of insight before. Which of the following have happened to you?

- You feel one with the cosmos on a starry summer night.
- You are struck by the generosity of spirit of an unexpected act of kindness.

- You feel a special sudden kinship with God during a service at your favorite place of worship.
- You benefit from the wisdom brought to you by a departed loved one in a dream.
- During a time of crisis, you are reminded that we are all in this together.
- The answer to a problem that has been worrying you appears out of the blue while you're in the shower.
- You are overcome with gratitude for the love in your life at a family gathering.
- You wonder anew at the miracle of life when you hold a newborn baby.
- Someone you thought would never forgive you for a past action reaches out to you, and you are humbled by the gesture.
- You forgive someone you thought you could never forgive, and you feel liberated by the gesture.

In Zen Buddhism, such a flash of awareness is called a *satori*. A satori can strike anytime, anywhere—all you have to do is notice it. When you are paying attention, life becomes a series of satori on the path to enlightenment.

MINDFULNESS: ENLIGHTENMENT WAITING TO HAPPEN

While we cannot plan to experience a satori, we can pay attention to our lives as we live them and become mindful of our aha! moments as they happen. Through mindfulness, we can set the stage to reconnect with spirit, illuminate our souls, and achieve enlightenment—one satori at a time.

From East to West, every tradition offers windows to our soul. Let us open these windows and let the light shine in.

What meditation is to the Eastern traditions, prayer is to the Western traditions. Indeed, there are more similarities than differences between these spiritual approaches. Both traditions seek the cultivation of silence as a meditative practice, and both share a desire for the peace of that meditative practice to influence our everyday lives.

What's more, they both aim to help us:

- Recognize the connections among heart, mind, and spirit
- Realize that divine energy or grace exists in and around the world of life
- Cultivate good character
- Discover a higher power through practice

In addition, the traditions that promote meditation or prayer offer a variety of approaches to unify heart, mind, and spirit, and they teach that divine energy or grace is accessible to us. It's not hard to see that the reasons for practicing them are shared by virtually every spiritual path. Only dogma separates them.

But, you might ask, isn't prayer directed to a separate entity and meditation directed to the self? Actually, the writings of Christian theologians resemble the teachings of the other traditions in many ways. Most important, the path to the higher power lies through the efforts of the individual alone. Only the route is different.

If we were to compare the approaches of meditation and prayer as paths on the journey from conscious existence to superconscious experience, it is really very simple. Meditation employs the mind; prayer employs the heart.

Prayer is a mindfulness tool that you can practice anywhere, anytime. You can call for divine grace, blessings, and assistance whenever you need to, and your reward will always be—in addition to whatever else—a mindful soul.

JESUS, TEACHER OF RIGHTEOUSNESS

Many mysteries surround the life and ministry of Jesus the Nazarene, born at the beginning of the Common Era in Bethlehem, Palestine. There are few details about his youth and education, but Jesus appeared at a critical time in Jewish history. Roman domination of the region had created immense hardship on its inhabitants. The Romans considered religious expression a threat to the supremacy of the Caesars, the emperors who had proclaimed themselves gods.

Jesus, a devout Jewish man, began a self-determined ministry at the age of thirty. At the time, there were several divisions in the Jewish faith. The orthodox Jews followed the strict dictates of the Sadducees, while the more liberal segment of society followed the Pharisees. A monastic tradition also existed. These followers, who lived separately in the region of the Dead Sea, away from the great cities, pursued a contemplative, mystical approach to Judaism. Many scholars believe that Jesus was a member of this movement. The Dead Sea Scrolls, found in 1947, were the records of this community and reveal provocative details about their beliefs. Among other things, they cite a "teacher of righteousness," who is believed to be Jesus. According to the scrolls, his role was to reveal the mysteries locked in the scriptures.

Ultimately, the life and death of Jesus became the fountainhead of a religious movement that changed the face of Western civilization. His two exhortations are the cornerstones of Christian doctrine: to love God above all other things and to love your neighbor as you love yourself.

"You shall love the Lord your God with all your heart and with all your soul and with all your mind. This is the great and first commandment. And a second is like it: You shall love your neighbor as yourself. On these two commandments depend all the Law and the Prophets."

— MATTHEW 22:37–40 ESV

LOVE IS THE ANSWER PRAYER

This is a prayer you can say as a mantra, recalling Jesus's challenge to love your neighbor as yourself:

Love is the answer.
Love is the answer.
Love is the answer.

THE GNOSTICS

In 1945, a cache of ancient papyrus scrolls was discovered in a remote region near Nag Hammadi, Egypt. After years of negotiating their ownership, scholars were able to determine that they dated from the fourth century. They were apparently copied from even older texts by a community of Christian ascetics known at the time as Gnostics ("those who know"). The term is also used to denote "insight."

The early Christian church regarded the Gnostics as heretics because their gospels were unauthorized by the early church. The Nag Hammadi scrolls are believed to be remnants of those gospels, and their contents have surprised and mystified scholars. They include teachings on spiritual practice and statements that closely resemble Buddhist thought. Excerpts have been compared to Zen koans.

A GNOSTIC KOAN

This is a divine riddle you can meditate on in times of trouble:

If you bring forth what is in you,
What you bring forth will save you.
If you do not bring forth what is within you,
What you do not bring forth will destroy you.

THE MONASTIC TRADITION

One of the first early Christians to formally retreat from society was a young man named Macarius, who began an austere life in Wadi Natrun in the western desert of Egypt. By the fourth century, the dissolution of the Roman Empire was under way, and many sought the peace and serenity that religious life offered. By the time Macarius passed away at the age of ninety, more than 4,000 monks had been drawn to his monastery alone. The movement was so widespread that a century later, the daughter of the Emperor Zeno joined the community disguised as a monk. After centuries of building, raids by a variety of rulers, and a renaissance in monastic life, the monastery of Macarius still flourishes today.

In the following centuries, from Egypt and the Sinai to Greece and westward to Europe, all classes of people joined these spiritual communities.

The Monk's Rule of Three

Monks (from the Greek *monos*, meaning "alone") initially lived in caves at the extremity of civilization. Their initial goal was threefold:

to reach *apatheia* ("pacification"), where the passions are quieted;

to practice *hesychia* ("reposing in silence"), where the mind withdraws from the outer world to reflect on spiritual realities; and

to attain *metanoia* ("all being together"), where the soul is transformed.

Monastic life followed a rule of order that dictated every daily activity. Prayer was the central practice throughout the day, punctuated only by domestic duties assigned to each member. Reflective time was also allotted to the study of scripture to provide inspiration. Guidelines were established that included poverty, chastity, and obedience. And, like the Buddhist monasteries, those of the Middle Ages "specialized," with a particular approach to emulating the life of Christ. Some were dedicated to healing the sick, others to teaching or preserving Christian writings.

THE CONTEMPLATIVES

Over time, withdrawal from the outside world became more than an accepted way to exercise the contemplative side of Christianity. The life of seclusion evolved into one of the few ways to receive an education or practice the arts. Gradually, those realms became intertwined with monastic life, so much so that the artistic and intellectual legacy of Western culture is innately connected to its spiritual tradition. The contemplative life encouraged this, and it is being revived today to encourage creative people to unlock their potential.

HILDEGARD OF BINGEN: THE POETESS OF PRAYER

Conditions in the eleventh century brought these circumstances to a summit. In 1098, Hildegard of Bingen was born to a noble family in what is now Germany. From childhood, she appeared to be unworldly, and she entered the religious life at fifteen. Until the age of forty-two, she pursued the contemplative regimen of the convent. Then she reported a revelatory vision, in which she understood "the meaning of the expositions of the books . . . the evangelists and other catholic books of the Old and New Testaments." More important, she also saw that her future work was to write about and expound on what she understood in her revelation.

The work and writings of Hildegard reflect that this revelation was more than an intuitive flash. She produced extensive theological works on Christian doctrine, poetry, music, and morality plays and scientific works on botany and medicine. She also presented a supremely meditative view on interpreting the Gospel of St. John. Seeing it as an allegory of the spiritual condition of the human race, she urged contemplation on spiritual rather than literal meanings of the Scriptures in her public teaching.

Hildegard did not go about her life quietly in a plain nun's habit, praying and contemplating throughout the day. Until her passing in 1179, she conducted herself as a resourceful manager of a convent, a composer, a teacher, and an artist. She is said to have worn colorful clothes and appreciated beautiful gems and scents. Her peers regarded her as prophetic and as one who saw profoundly into the mystical dimension of nature.

A CREATIVITY POEM

This is a prayer you can say whenever you feel the need for divine inspiration:

The earth is at the same time mother,
She is mother of all that is natural, mother of all that is human.
She is the mother of all, for contained in her are the seeds of all.
The earth of humankind contains all moistness, all verdancy,
All germinating power.
It is in so many ways fruitful.
All creation comes from it.
Yet it forms not only the basic raw material for mankind,
But also the substance of the incarnation of God's son.

—Hildegard of Bingen

ST. FRANCIS OF ASSISI: THE NATURE OF PEACE

In the thirteenth century, despite an early life of privilege and ease, a young Italian named Francesco di Bernadone received a spiritual command through prayer to dedicate his life to peace and contemplation. In answer to this, he was to found the brotherhood of the "little friars." They came to play a significant role in European spirituality in the following centuries as the Franciscans.

A former knight, Francesco began a new life in Assisi to live in imitation and union with Christ. Besides preaching and cultivating an attitude of equanimity with men and nature, he lived in poverty. When critics of the Church admonished him, he argued that he was truly free.

Ultimately, he was a man of God, a man of nature, and a man of peace.

A NATURE PRAYER

This is a prayer that celebrates the natural world and our place in it. Say it whenever you feel the grace of God in the bounty of nature.

Praised be you my Lord, with all your creatures,
Especially my Lord Brother Sun,
Who brings the day, and by whom you enlighten us.
He is beautiful, he shines with great splendor;
Of you, Most High, he is the symbol.
Praised be you, my Lord, for Sister Moon and the stars,

In the heavens you formed them clear, precious, and beautiful.
Praised be you, my Lord, for Brother Wind and for the air and for the clouds,
For the azure calm and for all climes by which you give life to your creatures.
Praised be you, my Lord, for Sister Water
Who is very useful and humble, humble and chaste.
Praised be you, my Lord, for Brother Fire,
By whom you enlighten the night.
He is beautiful and joyous, indomitable and strong.
Praised be you, my Lord, for our Mother the Earth
Who nourishes us and bears us, and produces all kinds of fruits,
With the speckled flowers and the herbs.

—St. Francis of Assisi

On his deathbed in 1226, it is reported that St. Francis repeated a last addition to this prayer: "Praised be you, my Lord, for our Sister Death."

LET PEACE BEGIN WITH ME PRAYER

This is a prayer to say whenever you are struggling to maintain peace in your world:

Lord, make me an instrument of your peace;
Where there is hatred, let me sow love;
Where there is injury, pardon;
Where there is doubt, faith;
Where there is despair, hope;
Where there is darkness, light;
And where there is sadness, joy.
Grant that I may not so much seek to be consoled as to console;
To be understood as to understand,
To be loved as to love.
For it is in giving that we receive,
It is in pardoning that we are pardoned,
And it is in dying that we are born to eternal life.

—St. Francis of Assisi

TERESA OF ÁVILA: THE BLESSING OF SILENCE

By the sixteenth century, monastic life for women was widespread in Europe. Influential intellects and mystics moved toward the contemplative life, away from the continually changing fortunes of political institutions throughout the region. Among them was a young Spanish woman, Teresa de Cepeda y Ahumada, born in 1515.

Although she became known for her reforms of the Carmelite order, St. Teresa's spiritual enlightenment emphasized a new concept: *oración mental*, the practice of mental prayer. Rather than a recitation, this was a kind of dialogue with God: "Mental prayer [oración mental] in my opinion is nothing else than a close sharing between friends; it means taking time frequently to be alone with Him who we know loves us."

St. Teresa passed away in 1582. Her works, *The Way of Perfection* and *The Interior Castle*, recount her teachings on mystical prayer to the sisters of her order. In 1970, she became the first woman to be named Doctor of the Church.

Call on the blessing of St. Teresa of Ávila whenever you need to connect with God in a personal way. Talk to God as if He were your friend, as she advised.

NIKODIMOS HAGIORITIS: THE PRAYER OF THE HEART

Nikodimos Hagioritis (1748–1809) was a Greek Orthodox monk who brought about a spiritual renaissance through his writings on "the love of the good and beautiful." He initially entered on this devotional path to translate the writings of the Eastern Orthodox Church, but on spiritual pilgrimages through Greece and Turkey, he discovered the "prayer of the heart." This is perpetual prayer, the continuous recitation of the name of Jesus. By performing this prayer constantly, Nikodimos taught that the mind would relinquish its attachment to the world and come to rest in the heart. Here, it is possible to enter the divine state.

This revelation is recorded in his prodigious work, the *Philokalia*. It was to later influence an anonymous Russian writer in the mid-nineteenth century who produced the classical spiritual novel, *The Way of a Pilgrim*. It recounts the journey of a seeker who attains spiritual realization by reciting the prayer, "Lord Jesus Christ, Son of God, have pity on me."

THE "OH, GOD!" PRAYER

They say that the shortest prayer is "Oh, God," which is in effect a prayer of the heart. The next time you say or hear someone else say "Oh, God," or something similar, turn that lament into a prayer of the heart.

THOMAS MERTON: POET OF THE LORD

In recent times, a renaissance of contemplative prayer emerged from the inspirational poetry and art of the Trappist monk Father Lewis, known to the public as Thomas Merton. Born in 1915, Merton came to the United States from France in the 1930s to study and teach. Although he had been agnostic in early life, he converted to Catholicism and left the teaching profession for a life of solitude as a monk. He chose the Trappists, the popular name for a branch of the Cistercian order founded in seventeenth-century France. Their rules are very strict—seclusion, minimal food, meatless diet, hard labor, and a vow of silence. However, that regimen has not prevented its members from pursuing artistic and social endeavors. In that spirit, Merton produced best-selling social commentaries and religious works in the form of prayers, poetry, and meditations.

The Abbey of Our Lady of Gethsemani, near Bardstown, Kentucky, became Merton's home, where he taught students and novices. He wrote about learning stillness through "centering prayer," and about a concept shared by many meditative paths, the "final integration." Merton believed that final integration brings every person in contact with his/her true nature, a divine nature.

Merton became a close friend of Thich Nhat Hanh, the Vietnamese Zen Buddhist monk who proposed the idea of engaged (socially active) Buddhism. Merton passed away in 1968 in Bangkok, Thailand, while attending an ecumenical conference of Buddhist and Christian monks. Today, Thomas Merton contemplative retreats are offered around the world, and a foundation disseminates his works and teachings.

PRAY IN A CHURCH

Whenever you pass by a church, drop in for five minutes, and say a prayer, as Thomas Merton advised. Let your soul sing while you pray.

THE SACRED HEART OF JESUS DEVOTION

Devotion to the Sacred Heart of Jesus began with St. Margaret Mary Alacoque (1647–1690), a nun of the Visitation order. According to Margaret Mary, Jesus appeared to her and offered his heart as a refuge for humankind, promising her that whoever kept an image of the heart visible in the home would be granted fulfillment of several promises. Among these promises were the fulfillment of material needs fitting to the person's station in life, peace in family matters, speed in the perfection of sanctity, and consolation in life and death.

THE SACRED HEART MEDITATION

Whenever you pray for a given outcome, call on the promise of a Sacred Heart devotion like the following:

Heart of Jesus, of infinite majesty, have mercy on us.
Heart of Jesus, holy temple of God, have mercy on us.
Heart of Jesus, house of God and gate of Heaven, have mercy on us.
Heart of Jesus, glowing furnace of charity, have mercy on us.
Heart of Jesus, full of goodness and love, have mercy on us.
Heart of Jesus, abyss of all virtues, have mercy.

THE MYSTERIES OF THE ROSARY

One of the most important Catholic devotions, increasingly practiced by other Christians as well, is the Rosary. The Rosary can be a fruitful way of prayer or meditation when you don't know what words to say or when meditating in silence becomes too difficult. The Rosary can also be a big help when you feel "stuck" in some particular life situation or spiritual problem.

The Rosary can be said in twenty or thirty minutes, or it can take hours. It all depends on the amount of time spent ruminating on each prayer. The scenes from Scripture can actually be read or simply recalled on the indicated beads. As for the rosary itself, you can buy a set of plastic beads for a few dollars or an ornate strand for hundreds of dollars. Try to purchase one that will not be so fragile that it breaks after one or two uses and can stand up to being placed in a pocket. Traditionally, a rosary should be blessed by a priest and should not be worn as jewelry. The Rosary can be said before a candle or an image of Jesus, Mary, or a favorite saint.

There are several prayers that are repeated as the Rosary is said:

APOSTLES' CREED

I believe in God, the Father Almighty, Creator of Heaven and earth, and in Jesus Christ, His only Son, our Lord, Who was conceived by the Holy Spirit, born of the Virgin Mary, suffered under Pontius Pilate, was crucified, died and was buried. He descended into Hell; the third day he arose again from the dead; He ascended into Heaven and is seated at the right hand of God the Father Almighty, from thence He shall come to judge the living and the dead. I believe in the Holy Spirit, the Holy Catholic Church, the Communion of Saints, the forgiveness of sins, the resurrection of the body, and life everlasting. Amen.

GLORY BE (GLORIA PATRI)

Glory be to the Father, and to the Son, and to the Holy Spirit, as it was in the beginning, is now, and ever shall be, world without end. Amen.

HAIL MARY

Hail Mary, full of grace, the Lord is with thee. Blessed art thou among women, and blessed is the fruit of thy womb, Jesus. Holy Mary, Mother of God, pray for us sinners, now and at the hour of our death. Amen.

OUR FATHER (THE LORD'S PRAYER)

Our Father, Who art in Heaven, hallowed be Thy Name. Thy Kingdom come. Thy Will be done, on earth, as it is in Heaven. Give us this day our daily bread and forgive us our trespasses as we forgive those who trespass against us; and lead us not into temptation, but deliver us from evil [for thine is the kingdom, and the power, and the glory forever]. Amen.

HAIL HOLY QUEEN

Hail Holy Queen, Mother of Mercy, our life, our sweetness, and our hope. To thee do we cry, poor banished children of Eve. To thee do we send up our sighs, mourning and weeping in this valley of tears. Turn then, most gracious advocate, Thine eyes of mercy toward us, and after this, our exile, show unto us the blessed fruit of thy womb, Jesus. O, clement, O loving, O sweet Virgin Mary. Pray for us O Holy Mother of God, that we may be worthy of the promises of Christ. Amen.

O MY JESUS

O my Jesus, forgive us our sins. Save us from the fires of hell. Lead all souls into heaven, especially those in most need of thy mercy. Amen.

MYSTERIES OF THE HOLY ROSARY			
JOYFUL MYSTERIES	SORROWFUL MYSTERIES	GLORIOUS MYSTERIES	LUMINOUS MYSTERIES
MONDAY AND SATURDAY	TUESDAY AND FRIDAY	WEDNESDAY AND SUNDAY	THURSDAY
1. The Annunciation	1. The Agony in the Garden	1. The Resurrection	1. The Baptism in the Jordan
2. The Visitation	2. The Scourging at the Pillar	2. The Ascension	2. The Wedding at Cana
3. The Birth of Jesus	3. The Crowning with Thorns	3. Coming of the Holy Ghost	3. The Proclamation of the Kingdom
4. The Presentation of Jesus in the Temple	4. The Carrying of the Cross	4. The Assumption of Mary into Heaven	4. The Transfiguration
5. The Finding of Jesus in the Temple	5. Crucifixion and Death of Jesus	5. The Crowning of Mary	5. The Institution of the Eucharist
Scripture: Luke 1–2	Matthew 26–27	John 20; Luke 24; Acts 2	Matthew 3, 17, 26

HOW TO SAY THE ROSARY

1. On the cross or crucifix, say the Apostles' Creed.
2. On the first bead, say the Our Father.
3. Say the Hail Mary three times.
4. On the last invitatory bead, say the Glory Be and announce the first mystery (Example: "The first mystery is The Baptism in the Jordan). Then say the Our Father.
5. Say the Hail Mary ten times while meditating on the first mystery.
6. On the next set, say the Glory Be, announce the second mystery, and say the Our Father.
7. Say ten Hail Marys. Repeat the process for the third, fourth, and fifth mysteries.
8. To conclude, say the Glory Be, O My Jesus, and Hail Holy Queen.

The Rosary is a meditative tour through the Gospel story as viewed through the eyes of Mary. Most people probably think of the Rosary as a Roman Catholic devotion, and that is its largest audience. But the words of the prayers themselves and the Gospel events in the mysteries are derived from Scripture and are important for all Christians. Those outside the Christian tradition may also find the prayers meaningful since Christ is, after all, a human being. His life and sufferings have something to do with all of us. If anyone can practice Zen meditation, why can't anyone say the Rosary?

5-MINUTE ROSARY MEDITATION

You don't have to wait until you have time to say the full Rosary. You can say the Rosary in five minutes when you simply recite the name of the prayer associated with each bead rather than say the entire prayer, as in Our Father, Hail Mary, Glory Be, etc. This honors each prayer as a mantra.

WALK THE LABYRINTH

The labyrinth is a medieval devotion, which has been revived in recent decades. An intricate geometric pattern originally built into the floor of a cathedral or carved into the doorframe at the entrance of a place of worship (for finger walking the labyrinth before entering), the labyrinth allows the faithful to make a metaphoric pilgrimage to Jerusalem without leaving home. The center of the circular pattern represents Jerusalem, and the seeker will reach the center by means of the circuitous pathway. The labyrinth is not a maze: The path will lead to the center and back out, and there are no dead ends or detours. Psychologically, though, the labyrinth plays on the walker's expectations, as the way that seems to be close to the center will often lead right back to the outer edge again.

If walked with intention, the labyrinth becomes a way of bodily prayer. It can become a complex form of introspection, or it can simply be a few minutes spent in silence. Students of religion will find the comparisons to yogic yantras and Tibetan mandalas to be striking. Though in former centuries, the center represented Jerusalem, it can also be seen as coming home to your own center. Places of worship in major metropolitan areas will often have a labyrinth available for walking, and portable versions, printed on canvas, are also available. Walking the labyrinth can be a good way to mark the beginning or end of a retreat, to prepare for a worship service or meditation group, or to get rid of nagging distractions and doubts. This deceptively simple traditional devotion will allow you to walk your way to your own center as you walk through the labyrinth.

"Pray, and let God worry."

— MARTIN LUTHER

CHAPTER 9
SUTRAS FOR YOUR SOUL

"Some perceive God in the heart by the intellect through meditation; others by the yoga of knowledge; and others by the yoga of work."

—BHAGAVAD GITA

Yoga is a philosophy designed to help you achieve enlightenment. Patanjali is credited with compiling the basic tenets of yoga philosophy into the *Yoga Sutras*.

THE MANY PATHS OF YOGA

Yoga has many paths. All lead to transformational growth and self-actu-alization; all are exercises in mindfulness.

RAJA YOGA

Raja means "royal." Its focus is meditation and contemplation. Many practitioners of Raja Yoga live in spiritual communities or religious orders.

5-Minute Raja

You don't have to become a monk or a nun to be part of a yoga community. Find a teacher and/or studio you like and attend classes. You can also attend workshops, festivals, and other yoga-related events, where you'll meet lots of people with whom you can share the yogic journey.

KARMA YOGA

Karma Yoga is the path of service. If you are alive, you're on the path of Karma Yoga. Because your life is a consequence of your past actions, you must learn to consciously make your decisions to create a future that is free from selfishness and negativity. You are practicing Karma Yoga whenever you perform a selfless service.

5-Minute Karma

Practice random acts of kindness. Doing something for someone else, especially a stranger in need, helps you feel gratitude for what you have and realize the difference between what you want and what you really need. That's karmic mindfulness in action.

BHAKTI YOGA

Bhakti Yoga is the path of the heart and devotion. A practitioner on this path sees the divine in everyone and everything and devotes his/her life to cultivating acceptance, love, and tolerance for all.

5-Minute Bhakti

Remember that the traditional yogic greeting *namaste* literally means "The divine in me honors the divine in you." Whenever someone annoys, insults, or challenges you, stop before you respond in kind. Honor the divine in the person, as you honor the divine in yourself. Find a way to approach him/her with love and compassion rather than with anger and irritation.

JNANA YOGA

Jnana Yoga is the yoga of the mind. Scholars who seriously study the yogic scriptures and texts are Jnana yogis.

HATHA YOGA

Hatha Yoga is the path of physical yoga. Physical postures, breathing techniques, deep relaxation, and meditation comprise Hatha Yoga.

TANTRA YOGA

Tantra Yoga is the path of ritual. It is the most misunderstood path. Part of the tantric path includes rituals for consecrated (or sacred) sexuality. Unfortunately, it is this aspect of Tantra Yoga that the media has publicized and blown out of proportion to seem more sexual than it really is. The practice of Tantra Yoga utilizes rituals to reverentially experience the sacred in *everything* we do, not just in sex. It is the most esoteric of all the yogas and attracts those who enjoy ceremony, celebration, and ritual.

THE *YOGA SUTRAS:* IT'S ALL ABOUT CLARITY

According to Patanjali, author of the influential *Yoga Sutras*, the goal of yoga is to reach the state of yoga called *samadhi*, where the mind is crystal clear and free from impressions of the past or thoughts of the future. This hallowed text addresses how we perceive things and explains why we are always getting into trouble in life.

According to Patanjali, it is our perceptions that color our view of reality and prevent us from clearly seeing the truth. If we cannot see a situation with clarity, we are unable to act accurately.

Patanjali says there are five main factors that interfere with our ability to see clearly and accurately:

- Comprehension
- Misapprehension
- Imagination
- Deep sleep
- Memory

Each of these can be beneficial when appropriate and in balance with our needs; otherwise, they can cause problems:

- Our mind fills with misapprehension and fear—and we fail to act
- We rely too much on our imagination and memory—and fail to see the simple truth right before our eyes
- We spend too much time asleep—literally and figuratively

But when you see something correctly, without interference, you feel a deep feeling of calmness and peace. Tension dissolves. Instability and agitation decrease. Over time, you experience longer periods of clarity of thought and emotional stability, your attitude shifts from negative thoughts and fear to positive thoughts and freedom, and you are able to maintain samadhi for longer periods of time.

THE EIGHT LIMBS OF YOGA

Patanjali uses the word *limb* to describe the different aspects of your yogic practice, which, when taken together, make up one body of yoga. The purpose of this eightfold path is to bring the mind, body, and spirit into harmony. Each limb can grow simultaneously or at different times. They develop together spontaneously in a process that is developmental, harmonious, and organic. The limbs are:

- **Yamas:** Your attitudes toward others outside of yourself or universal laws
- **Niyamas:** Your attitude about yourself or your personal observances
- **Asanas:** Physical postures
- **Pranayama:** Regulation and control of the breath
- **Pratyahara:** Withdrawal of the senses
- **Dharana:** Concentration
- **Dhyana:** Meditation
- **Samadhi:** Self-realization or enlightenment

These limbs are not sequential rungs of a ladder that must be climbed from bottom to top. You can begin with any limb and experience the other limbs at any time. All the limbs lead to the same destination, samadhi.

YAMAS: UNIVERSAL LAWS

The yamas are the roots of the tree of yoga. They provide the foundation for the practice.

AHIMSA

The first yama is *ahimsa*. Ahimsa means "nonharming, nonviolence." But it is much more than that. To observe ahimsa is to practice kindness, friendliness, and thoughtfulness toward others and yourself. Ahimsa includes observing whether your thoughts and actions are leading to your personal growth and the welfare of all beings. It is about living life peacefully without fear. Some may interpret ahimsa as not eating meat, not wearing animal skins, and so on, but these are a matter of personal preference and decision.

Not harming yourself and others could also mean providing food and shelter for your family and physically defending yourself from danger. Each circumstance must be acted on independently and with flexibility of thought and awareness, while keeping the principles of ahimsa in your mind.

START WITH YOU! EXERCISE

Ahimsa isn't just about your treatment of others. You would be practicing ahimsa when doing yoga postures in a way that did not cause injury or harm to *yourself*. Honoring the body's needs at each moment in time, listening and responding appropriately, is practicing ahimsa. This means not pushing beyond your range of comfort. The next time you find yourself pushing yourself too hard in any situation, stop—and practice ahimsa.

SATYA

The next yama is *satya*, or "truthfulness." Satya means "to speak the truth." However, it is not always possible to speak the truth because the truth may be harmful to another person. It is important to think before you speak and to consider the consequences of your words. If speaking the truth would be destructive to another person, it might be better to say nothing rather than tell a lie. Gossiping can be considered harmful to the person receiving it. In this way, satya would be in alignment with the principle of ahimsa (nonharming).

Satya can be seen as living a truthful life that is in alignment with your own needs and abilities. People who are unhappy with their job, marriage, or relationship are not living their life in accordance with satya.

LIVE YOUR TRUTH! EXERCISE

Make a list of all the ways you are living your truth—and all the ways you are not. Come up with strategies to get back on track where you've strayed from your truth.

ASTEYA

Asteya is the third yama. It means "nonstealing" or "not taking what does not belong to us." Asteya refers to nonstealing of material things, as well as of other's ideas. If someone confides in you, it would be appropriate to keep the confidence rather than break it by telling someone else the confidential information.

Asteya encompasses misappropriation, mismanagement, and mistrust and involves the misuse of power. Using power in a way that is self-serving rather than for the good of others would not be practicing asteya. Machiavelli's "the end justifies the means" is not in accordance with asteya.

KEEP A SECRET! EXERCISE

It's not easy to keep a secret, even our own. When was the last time that you betrayed a confidence? Whom did it hurt most—the person with the secret or you? Or both?

BRAMACHARYA

The fourth yama is *bramacharya*, which means "to move toward the essential truth." Bramacharya has commonly been seen as self-control, abstinence, or moderation, especially regarding sexual activity. Sexual energy is more than the act of sexual union and those activities related to it. It is the creative power of each person.

Celibacy has been thought of as bramacharya, but it is really moderation of the senses and desires that is most important. Bramacharya is about conserving your creative energies so they are not dissipated.

The *Yoga Sutras* caution that giving into the ego's excessive desires can lead us far off the path of yoga. We are told that it is responsible behavior that moves us to our truth. Remember the second statement of the Delphi oracles: "Nothing in excess." This also applies to our yoga practice. Life should be full of health, balance, and harmony.

CONTROL YOURSELF! EXERCISE

When was the last time you overindulged in alcohol, food, or sex? What prompted you to do so? How can you avoid making the same mistake again?

APARIGRAHA

Aparigraha, the last yama, means "to take only what is necessary and not to take advantage of someone or of a situation." It implies nonhoarding and faith and trust in what life has to offer each one of us. We are asked to take what we have fairly earned, not to ask for an excessive amount for our efforts. It is about learning to live a simple, contented life, satisfied with what you have and believing that you will be given all that you need. Aparigraha refers to correctly and appropriately using one's power, not exploiting someone else. It is all about correct use of power.

OWN YOUR POWER! EXERCISE

Think of a time when you used your power unwisely—at work, at home, in the world at large. Meditate on the nature of aparigraha. How would you handle things differently today?

NIYAMAS: PERSONAL OBSERVANCES

The second limb of yoga is the *niyamas*. They are personal observances toward ourselves. Niyamas are the trunk of the tree of yoga. They control the senses of perception: the eyes, ears, nose, mouth and tongue, and skin.

SAUCHA

The first niyama is *saucha*, or "cleanliness." Saucha implies both inner and outer cleanliness of our internal and external environments. Inner cleanliness is of utmost importance for preserving the healthy functioning of every body system. The physical postures, breathing techniques, and yogic cleansing practices irrigate and detoxify the physical body.

The mind must also be kept clean. Holding onto old thoughts and ways of perceiving can clutter the mind, making it difficult to think clearly. Spring cleaning of the mind is needed.

TRATAKA: GAZING EXERCISE

Gazing, or *trataka*, encompasses a number of practices that involve focusing on an object, such as a candle, for an extended length of time. This practice results in an increased ability to focus one's attention and purify the mind. The next time you find yourself unable to calm your monkey mind, light a candle and gaze into it. Focus on the flame, breathe deeply, center yourself, and connect to your soul. Breathe in peace; breathe out angst. Repeat.

SAMTOSHA

Samtosha, the second niyama, means being modest, humble, and content with who we are and with what we have in this life. Samtosha also means to accept what happens in life rather than rigidly pursuing a specific goal or an expectation of how things are supposed to be. Samtosha is all about enjoying the process and the journey through life, taking time to smell the roses. This includes practicing yoga in a process-oriented way, not as a goal-directed activity.

AN EXERCISE IN HUMILITY

Remember the last time life humbled you. What were the circumstances? Why did you feel humbled? What lesson in samtosha can you learn from this?

TAPAS: A BURNING DESIRE FOR WHOLENESS

Tapas means "to heat or cleanse." Tapas in the *Yoga Sutras* refers to the practice of physical postures and breathing exercises, which are designed to heat you up and rinse you clean. They help you release blocks and impurities from the mind and the body, in addition to providing many benefits. In the larger sense, tapas also refers to the burning desire toward wholeness, self-knowledge, and self-integration that characterizes the mindful individual.

"WHO AM I?" EXERCISE

How well do you really know yourself? Think of the last thing you did that surprised you. When was the last time you asked yourself, "Why/how did I do that?" In what way was it seemingly "uncharacteristic" of you? Why so? Is it an action you'd want to repeat? If so, why? If not, why not? Meditate on these questions, and in the process, become more mindful of who you are and who you were meant to be.

SVADHYAYA: KNOW THYSELF

Through *svadhyaya*, we examine and rediscover our true selves. The reading of yoga scriptures and texts helps with this self-study. We also observe our thoughts, actions, and reactions when doing yoga, as well as in daily life.

"WHAT COMES UP" EXERCISE

Often when we do yoga, we find ourselves overcome with emotion. We grow bored, restless, resistant, irritated, fatigued, frustrated, or even sad, angry, or ecstatic. Whenever this happens to you, note your feelings—and delve into them. Why do you think you react in a particular way? What posture are you in, what music is playing, what are you thinking about? How do all these things interrelate?

ISHVARA PRANIDHANA: SURRENDERING TO THE INFINITE

Ishvara pranidhana speaks to the surrender and devotion required to fully commit to the path of yoga. This surrender happens again and again as your practice deepens—and your self-actualization grows. Practicing postures and breathing techniques, along with self-study, is not enough to reach enlightenment. You must continue living your daily life, working and living with others in a way that is positive and loving.

Ishvara pranidhana means "to lay all your actions at the feet of God." As we grow in awareness, and experience the unpredictability of life, we realize that we are really not in control and we need to surrender our lives and our false sense of control to whatever gives us a sense of wholeness and sacredness, whether that be in the form of God or nature. Offering prayer is a way of acknowledging the role of ishvara pranidhana in our lives. Twelve-step programs, such as Alcoholics Anonymous and Overeaters Anonymous, have integrated this niyama into their program and belief system.

"SURRENDER" EXERCISE

The next time you find yourself resisting what is happening in your life—on the mat or off—surrender to it. If you're struggling to meet the challenge of a pose, give up and relax into the stretch. If you're strug-gling to meet the challenge of a job or a relationship, give up and relax into the stretch your job or your relationship is asking you to make.

ASANA: PHYSICAL POSTURES

The third limb of yoga is *asana*, the physical postures that relax, rejuvenate, strengthen, and energize the body. While doing the pos-tures of yoga, you focus on the breath. The breath is your connection to feeling prana, your life force. And, as you move through the postures, you are helping to loosen tension and create space for prana to more easily flow throughout the body. That is why certain yoga postures are ideal for energy healing: They can help release blocks by creating space for energy to flow in places that may have been blocked. When you unblock energy flow, you create health.

CHAKRAS AND THE ASANAS

Chakra is Sanskrit for "wheel of light." The chakras are energy cen-ters, likened to spinning vortexes, that conduct electromagnetic energy. Each of the seven major chakras in the body relates to the physical and subtle energy bodies that make up your entire being. You are more than your physical body. You have all of these "bodies": the physical body, the mental body, the emotional body, the intellectual body, the astral body, the etheric body, and the ketheric body. The astral body, located at the heart center, is the bridge between matter and spirit. It is the inte-gration of these seven bodies that occurs in yoga.

There are seven main chakras, or energy centers, in the subtle body, located along the spine, and 122 smaller chakras throughout the body. The seven chakras correspond to the major glands in the physical body, to major nerve plexuses, and to specific colors, depending on the fre-quency that each chakra spins.

Each chakra in the subtle body is recognized as a concentrated point of life force, relating to physical, emotional, mental, and spiritual energies.

The smaller chakras are located where bones, joints, and secondary nerve plexuses meet. They are a network through which the body, mind, and spirit interact. The seven chakras are:

- **Muladhara:** The root chakra, found between the pubic bone and the base of the spine and associated with the gonads, is the seat of the physical body and is emotionally connected to basic issues of survival, such as food, shelter, and security. It spins at the frequency of the color red.

- **Swadhistana:** Located near the lumbosacral plexus, behind and below the navel, the second chakra corresponds to the reproductive glands (the ovaries and prostate) and is the center of the emotional body, where your feelings about yourself, sexuality, and others are felt. The color of this chakra is orange.

- **Manipura:** The third chakra, found at the solar plexus in the "V" formed by the ribs, below the chest and above the navel, is related to the adrenal glands and the spleen and is the seat of the mental body, where thinking and gut feelings occur. Yellow is the color frequency of this chakra.

- **Anahata:** The fourth chakra, located at the brachial plexus midway between the two breasts, is called the heart chakra (associated with the thymus gland, sometimes called the *high heart*) and is the home of the astral body, considered to be the bridge between the physical and spiritual planes. It deals with issues of unconditional love, health, healing, acceptance, and forgiveness. The color of this chakra is green.

- **Vishudda:** The next chakra, related to the parathyroid and thyroid glands, is found at the base of the throat and is the etheric body, concerned with speaking one's personal truth, clear communication, and creative expression. The color frequency of vishudda is blue.

- **Ajna:** The sixth chakra, commonly called the *third eye*, is located between the eyebrows and connected to the pineal gland. It is the celestial body and is related to clarity of thought and sight, as the opening of this chakra allows for broader vision and perspective, such as a flying eagle's panoramic view of the world. Purple is the color of this chakra. It is interesting to note that the pope and members of royalty commonly wear this color.

- **Sahasrara:** The last chakra is the crown chakra, found just above the crown of the head. It is the ketheric body and is associated with the pituitary gland. Issues of unity, consciousness, and interconnectedness with all things comprise the seventh chakra, which is the place of samadhi, or enlightenment. Its color frequency is white.

The ancient chakra system is another way of understanding and connecting to the intelligence of the body, mind, and spirit. In each yoga pose, a variety of chakras are stimulated, leading to a balanced flow of energy throughout all systems and feelings of well-being.

YAMAS, NIYAMAS, AND CHAKRAS			
CHAKRA	QUALITY	YAMA	NIYAMA
Root	Nongrasping and Cleanliness	Aparigraha	Saucha
Sacral	Appropriate Use of Energy and Contentment	Bramacharya	Santosha
Solar Plexus	Manage Inner Fire		Tapas
Throat	Integrity	Satya	
Heart	Nonviolence	Ahimsa	
Third Eye	Clarity and Intuition	Self-Study	Svadyaya
Crown	Connection to Divine	Ishvara Pranidhana	

Practicing the yamas and niyamas will nurture the chakras. When you practice aparigraha, you are strengthening your belief that you have enough, that you are provided with what you need. You are safe and secure, and these are the issues of the root chakra. Saucha also supports your root chakra. Purity of your bodily systems, including skin and muscles, supports the Muladhara energy.

Bramacharya and santosha support the sacral chakra, whose issues are around energy and emotions. Tapas supports your solar plexus chakra. Satya supports the throat chakra. Speaking your truth and being in integrity strengthen this energy center.

Ahimsa supports the heart: Nonviolence to yourself and others cultivates the kind of love that emanates from here. Svadyaya brings energy to the third eye. At the third eye, you are connecting to your wisdom, combining what you learn through study and what you know with intuition. Ishvara pranidhana is the energy of the crown chakra, your connection in the universal intelligence that creates life and vitality.

COLOR VISUALIZATION FOR THE CHAKRAS

You can do visualizations anywhere, anytime when you can be still and focus your energy on the visualization.

Note: Don't do visualizations while you're driving because your focus should be on driving. Be focused. The power of the visualization is diluted if you are multitasking, watching TV, cooking dinner, etc.

For visualization, close your eyes and take a few deep, nourishing breaths. You can lie down, stand, or sit upright. Then, put your awareness on each chakra one at a time. While your awareness is at each level, breathe in and out a few times until you can envision the color of that chakra in that part of your body. Use the rainbow as your color guide.

- At the root chakra, envision red.
- At the sacral chakra, envision orange.
- At the solar plexus chakra, envision yellow.
- At the heart chakra, envision green.
- At the throat chakra, envision blue.

- At the third-eye chakra, envision indigo.
- At the crown chakra, envision white, violet, or gold.

Start at the root chakra. Take slow, deep breaths in and out, and with your imagination, connect to the perineum, where the energy center is located. After a few natural breaths, as you breathe this time, imagine inhaling red light into the root chakra. Hold in your breath for a few seconds, imagining the colored light sustained there. Exhale and let go. Do this three times, then move up to the sacral chakra and repeat the exercise, visualizing the color orange.

Continue up the chakras to the third eye, following the same pattern. When you finish with the third-eye visualization, let your breath naturally flow in and out. Imagine your crown chakra glowing white light that envelops your entire body and expands upward, connecting you to the wide expanse. After doing this for a few moments, release the visualization. Cross your arms in front of you, hugging yourself across your chest or waist. Feel the parts of you that are connected to the earth, grounding into the earth. Bring your awareness back into your body. And, when you feel complete, open your eyes.

PRANAYAMA: CONTROL OF BREATH

Pranayama is the fourth limb of yoga. In Sanskrit, *prana* is the cosmic energy that manifests in the breath. *Ayama* means expansion, increase. So pranayama is the process in which the prana is developed and strengthened in the body, purifying the nervous system and increasing the person's vital life energy.

As we have seen, the deep breathing of pranayama calms and focuses the mind. It is the combination of asana and pranayama that prepares us for deeper levels of concentration and consciousness by refining and strengthening the nervous system and the body's subtle energy.

PRATYAHARA: WITHDRAWAL OF THE SENSES

The next limb of yoga is *pratyahara*. It is the bark of the tree of yoga, which protects the tree, insulating it from the outside elements and enabling the inner energy to flow unimpeded. As the mind begins to calm and the attention settles, an inward focus is possible, no longer distracted by external events. The sense organs (eyes, ears, nose, mouth, skin) draw in from the periphery to the core to observe the inner world.

Pratyahara occurs when you are so totally absorbed in an activity that you become unaware of outside stimulation. You could be in the middle of Grand Central Station in New York City without seeing, hearing, smelling, feeling, or tasting anything.

IN THE ZONE

Immersed in a yoga pose, you become totally focused on the breath and the internal actions of the pose. Athletes commonly call this state "being in the zone." Here the process of self-discovery and evolution, with the body as the experimental laboratory, continues at a more refined level.

DHARANA: CONCENTRATION

The ability to focus without distraction leads to the next limb of yoga called *dharana*. Dharana is the sap of the tree of yoga, carrying the energy and the concentration deeper inside the individual. Dharana is the one-pointed, steady focus of the mind on one object at a time. Extended periods of concentration lead to meditation.

THE TOOTHBRUSH EXERCISE

It is possible to begin the practice of dharana with simple everyday activities. Focus on brushing your teeth. Observe how the bristles on the toothbrush move back and forth against your teeth, how the toothpaste tastes. This is *mindfulness*. There are abundant opportunities to practice it all day long.

DHYANA: MEDITATION

Meditation, or *dhyana*, is the seventh limb of yoga. It is the flowers of the tree of yoga, the blooming of the focused mind. Dhyana is the uninterrupted flow of concentration. This is different from the previous stage of dharana, as the ability to focus has been honed to the point where the concentration lasts for prolonged periods of time, without the one-pointed focus. Instead, the focus is expanded throughout the individual's consciousness. The mind has grown quiet, thoughts are at a minimum, and the experience is one of stillness.

The mindfulness state we achieve with meditation serves as a counterbalance to our crazy, busy lives—and sets the stage for enlightenment.

SAMADHI: ENLIGHTENMENT

The last limb of yoga is *samadhi*. It is the fruit of the tree of yoga, the harvest or reward of dedicated yoga practice. Samadhi has been variously described as a state of ecstasy, enlightenment, and a transcending of everyday reality, where you commune with the divine and interconnect with all living beings. This is a state of peace and completion, expanded awareness, and compassion with detachment (being *in* the world but not *of* it). Have you experienced moments of ecstasy or flashes of insight and knowingness that go beyond our smaller daily lives? Those aha! moments are a taste of samadhi.

"Regulate the breath, be happy, link the mind with the Lord in your heart."

— KRISHNAMACHARYA

CHAPTER 10
BE A MINDFUL MYSTIC

*"We have come into this exquisite world to experience ever and ever
more deeply our divine courage, freedom and light!"*

—HAFIZ

Mysticism is a spiritual path by which we achieve direct communion
with the transcendent, or ultimate reality, or God. Regardless of tradition, it's a path you follow by heart rather than intellect. Mystics call
on the power of images, music, chanting, dance, poetry, and more to
encourage and enhance this mystical union with the divine.

In this chapter, we'll explore the many ways in which we can call
on the mystical practices from a number of traditions to live a more
mindful life.

SUFIS AND THE WHIRLING DERVISH

Sufism is the mystical branch of Islam. The first Sufis date back to
the first century, following the Hegira, or flight of Mohammed from
Mecca to Medina in 622. Their name is derived from the Arabic *suf*
("wool") because they wore white woolen robes. The movement came
into being as a reaction against the warrior cult of the Umayyads. The
Sufis chose a mystical path and moved toward an esoteric interpreta-
tion of Islam.

Despite its mystical approach, in Sufism there is a science of achieving unity with God that is the central aim of the practice. It is outlined in three stages:

1. **Sair ita Allah: Progress toward God, which leads to** *fana*
2. **Sair fi Allah: Progress within God, which includes the experience of divine unity and acquiring divine attributes in the process, which is** *baqa*
3. **Sair 'ani Allah: Progress beyond God, which is attainment of nonexistence, the permanent state of fana**

The third stage cannot be approached through study or teachings. It can only be approached through direct experience, which has four components:

1. **Dhikr: Chanting the name of God**
2. **Riyadat: Ascetic practices such as fasting**
3. **Inkisar: Detachment from worldly things and conditions**
4. **Subha: Surrendering the ego to the absolute reality**

The poet Rumi advocated the calling of the divine name as the supreme approach to awakening the divine presence within. In the Sufi tradition, this is performed in conjunction with rhythmic breathing.

FIVE PURIFICATIONS OF THE SOUL EXERCISE

The exercise that prepares you for rhythmic breathing is the five purifications of the soul. The universal elements are the focal points, being earth, water, fire, and air. Begin at sunrise if possible, when the elements are at their peak. Stand upright.

Breathe slowly and deeply, keeping in mind the energy of the earth. Visualize it as the color yellow, entering your body as you inhale through the nose. The earth element travels upward from the ground, through your spine to your crown. As it does so, the earth filters out all impurities. It returns to the ground when you exhale through the nose. Repeat this four more times.

Breathe slowly and deeply, keeping in mind the energy of water. Visualize it as the color green, entering your nose as you inhale. The water element moves upward from the stomach, through your spine to your crown. As it does so, the liquid washes away all impurities. It exits from your stomach when you exhale through the mouth. Repeat this four more times.

Breathe slowly and deeply, keeping in mind the energy of fire. Visualize it as the color red, entering your body through your heart as you inhale. The fire element moves upward to your crown. As it does so, the fire burns away all impurities. It exits from your heart when you exhale through the nose. Repeat this four times (a total of five).

Breathe slowly and deeply, keeping in mind the energy of air. Visualize it as the color blue, entering your body through all of your pores as you inhale. The air element moves through all the organs and tissues, blowing away all the impurities. It exits through the pores when you exhale through your mouth. Repeat this four times (a total of five).

Invoke the Name of God

Following the breathing purifications, recite the divine name. In Islam, the names of God are manifold, but there is only one God. This dictate is cited in the Qu'ran and becomes the Sufi mantra for awakening the divine presence within: "There is no God but God: and Muhammad is his prophet" (*La ilaha illa-llah: Mohammedan rasul Allah*).

EXPERIENCE THE DIVINE

Sufism is an expression similar to Bhakti Yoga, the experience of seeing the divine presence in everything and honoring that divinity. There is simplicity in this approach, along with a rich and resonant love that transcends (but also includes) the personal realm. However, the

Sufis depart from the Bhakti Yoga tradition in that they do not revere gurus or teachers. Rather, they seek truth within themselves. Only angels can guide them.

> *"Melt yourself down in his search:*
> *venture your life and your soul*
> *in the path of sincerity;*
> *strive to pass from nothingness to being,*
> *and make yourself drunk with the wine of God."*
>
> —*Hakim Sanai*

THE WHIRLING DERVISH OF THE SOUL

In the West, Sufi dancing—also known as dance of the whirling dervishes—has drawn considerable interest. There is some hesitation, however, for women to participate due to the traditionally segregated nature of Islam. Even though women played a significant role in the life of Muhammad, prevailing customs keep much of the practice separated for men and women.

Unless you are a member of a Sufi *tariqa*, the modern experience of Sufism is limited to viewing dervish performances in theaters and events in some Muslim countries. Participation by outsiders is limited, although spiritual pilgrims are always welcomed.

ECSTATIC DANCE, USA

Here in the West, a movement called Dances of Universal Peace was established in the 1960s to explore Sufi dancing as a meditative art form.

The program of Dances of Universal Peace seeks to unite participants of all religious persuasions in the experience of sacred dance. A typical gathering begins with a rhythmic walking meditation in a circle to unify the participants in mind. Then, music accompanies simple dances around the circle. There is an emphasis on meeting with each person in the circle through turning and greeting. This is an important aspect of acknowledging the oneness of all present.

Dance of the Divine Exercise

Sacred dance is not a new idea, and many indigenous cultures use dance as a major component in their practices. The fusion of the senses with mind can allow you to transcend ordinary consciousness and enter exalted states of mind and feeling.

You can do your own version of ecstatic dance at any time. Put on some music that inspires you—kirtan, African tribal music, folk music, etc.—and let yourself go.

Mantras or phrases of sacred names are also incorporated into the modern Sufi dances. There are recitations of the many words for God: Allah, Yeshua (Jesus), Buddha, and Rama (among many others). The recitations are chanted to the rhythm of the music.

Many nondenominational groups around the world now sponsor Dances of Universal Peace on a recurring basis. There are local chapters in some major U.S. cities, and events are held at Unitarian churches and on university campuses.

There are also dance experiences offered at yoga and retreat centers around the country by yoga and movement teachers who guide you to experience the healing, fun, and ecstatic rhythms of life through music and dance. These events, classes, or workshops vary in how much the teacher leads and how much you are free to move around the space in any way you want. JourneyDance, YogaDance, Soul Motion, Shake Your Soul, and 5 Rhythms are some of the numerous options out there. There's bound to be a teacher and event near you. You could pop in for one class or sign up for a whole workshop or teacher training and dance, dance, dance.

THE SIKHS: A FUSION OF MYSTICAL TRADITIONS

In the fifteenth century, a religious teacher in what is now Pakistan attempted to remedy the segregation of the sexes and classes in religious practice. In addition, he also sought to reconcile the prevailing religions of his day: Islam, Hinduism, and Buddhism. Guru Nanak founded the Sikh ("disciple") movement, a mystical sect that practiced trance meditation and believed in one God and harmonious living.

Nanak wrote the *Jap-ji*, a collection of poems that is now the Sikh guiding principle. He spoke of union with the divine presence and methods by which it could be realized. His spiritual approach was a fusion of Bhakti Yoga and Tantra Yoga with Sufism. One of the mantras of the practice expresses this cohesion:

Eck Ong Kar Sat Nam Siri Wha Guru.
The Supreme is One, His names are many.

THE FIVE ELEMENTS MEDITATION

Sikhs also recognize the elemental forces that Sufism presents, although they are associated with qualities of mind:

Earth teaches us patience and love;
Air teaches us mobility and liberty;
Fire teaches us warmth and courage;
Sky teaches us equality and broadmindness;
Water teaches us purity and cleanliness.
We will imbibe these qualities in Nature
For our personalities to be fuller, happier, and nobler.

"One who is absorbed in the Beloved and has renounced all else is a Sufi."

—NAJM AD-DIN KUBRA

THE MANDALA: A BUDDHIST AND HINDU TRADITION

"The mandala is an archetypal image whose occurrence is attested throughout the ages. It signifies the wholeness of the self. This circular image represents the wholeness of the psychic ground or, to put it in mythic terms, the divinity incarnate in man."

—CARL JUNG

The mandala ("circle") is a diagram that can feature images of deities, plants, and animals. Each image has a symbolic meaning that represents certain qualities. The mandala conveys synthesis and integration, showing the relationships that exist between the elements in the image and ourselves. Concentric circles are used to depict levels or layers of reality, symbolizing our journey into the inner realms. In this respect, the mandala is also a map of those regions.

In the Buddhist tradition, mandalas are viewed as magical objects. With practice, you may "absorb" the qualities of the image and, through the process, receive healing or special illuminations.

Mandalas are sometimes three dimensional. In the Tibetan tradition, these images are created from dyed sand and plant materials, such as rice and seeds. They are carefully arranged in intricate designs on floors, tables, and cushions for special ceremonies. When the event is over, the materials are gathered and returned to nature.

COLOR YOUR MANDALA EXERCISE

You can create your own mandala or download one from the Internet to color. There are free ones at sites such as *www.coloringcastle.com* you can use, or you can buy one of the many mandala coloring books available at bookstores and at *www.amazon.com*. This is also a fun mindfulness project to do with kids of all ages.

Yantras are drawn on walls, curtains, and tablets that are placed in the meditation environment. A limited number of colors are used; each color symbolizes a particular state of mind and cosmic activity.

The Yogic Yantra

The yogic equivalent of the mandala is the *yantra* ("support"), a linear diagram that supports a visualization. It is usually geometric and symmetrical, combining circles with squares and joining the lines inside and outside each figure. This design conveys the idea of order, harmony, and balance. The yantra is used for centering, and in tantric practice, it is believed to offer protection. You place your conscious presence in the center, where it is "shielded" from interferences of thought and feeling.

JUDAISM AND THE TREE OF LIFE

"Blessed are they that do his commandments, that they may have right to the tree of life, and may enter in through the gates into the city."

—REVELATION 22:14

Judaism arose more than 4,000 years ago in what is now the State of Israel as a divine covenant between God and the ancient Hebrews. Like every religion, Judaism is mostly known by its orthodox dogma and practices, but it also has an esoteric dimension. It is outlined in the Kabbalah ("tradition"), the third book of Judaism that provides the contemplative vehicle of the tradition. It is a body of knowledge that discloses the structure of the universe and its relation to human consciousness.

The Kabbalah itself consists primarily of two texts, which reveal the esoteric tradition of Israel. They are the *Sepher Yetzirah* (*Book of*

Formation) and the *Sepher ha Zohar* (*Book of Splendor*). They date from the second century and, in the Middle Ages, were carried to Europe, where medieval philosophers added appendices with numerous commentaries. These were revived in the early-twentieth century by metaphysical movements in Europe, particularly the Order of the Golden Dawn and, in America, by the Theosophists.

THE TREE OF LIFE

The essence of kabbalistic teaching is the *Otz Chiim* ("tree of life"). It is a sort of master plan of the universe, but it is also a map through the inner worlds that guides the mystic traveler. The Tree of Life is a meditative image, a mandala of the universe and the soul in one symbol. Recalling the narrative in Genesis of the Tree of Knowledge of Good and Evil, the story may be viewed as an allegory of the separation of spirit and matter when physical life came into being. The reunion of those two worlds is the goal of the meditator in this system. It is accomplished by following the "paths" that are outlined in the Tree of Life.

There are ten individual *sephira* ("worlds") that comprise the Tree of Life. They are arranged in three vertical rows, or "pillars," representing the three modes of approach. Those modes are active, passive, and modulating. The meditator is guided as much as possible upward, through the middle path, or pillar. This approach avoids extremes of mental and emotional experience.

Going up through the worlds in the Tree of the Sephiroth, the meditator also moves through four levels, or planes, of cosmic activity: *Assiah*, *Yetzirah*, *Briah*, and *Aziluth*. These are, progressing upward, the states of physical life, angelic life (nature spirits included), the created universe (celestial bodies and forces), and the region of divine beings, respectively. They also symbolize layers of consciousness.

Let's look at the individual worlds of the Sephirothic Tree to understand this view of the meditative path.

- We begin in the state of *Assiah* ("physical life") and first encounter *Malkuth* ("the kingdom"), the entry gate on the path to illumination. In this world are the four elements. Their colors are citrine, brown, and gray. This is where the body exists and the natural world finds expression.
- From *Assiah*, we enter the state of *Yetzirah* ("immaterial life"). In *Yesod* ("the foundation"), we encounter the tidal ebb and flow, the region of shadowy images that mirror life in the material world. The color is purple. *Hod* ("splendor") is where we discover luminous perception, a clarity of thought and the senses. The color is orange. In *Netzach* ("victory"), the world of harmony and achievement is experienced. The color is green.
- From *Yetzirah*, we enter the state of *Briah* ("the cosmic world"). *Tipareth* ("beauty") is the central Sun, the illumination of nature's source. The color is yellow. *Geburah* ("severity") is the solar system, a tightly wound mechanism of matter and energy in motion. The color is red. *Chesed* ("mercy") is the galaxies, ever-expanding clusters of stars that are born and die in eons of time. The color is blue.
- From *Briah*, we come into the state of *Aziluth* ("divine consciousness"). *Binah* ("understanding") is the cosmic mother, where creation is brought forth. The color is violet. *Chokmah* ("wisdom") is the cosmic father, where the impulse of life emanates. The color is indigo. *Kether* ("the crown") is the source of all creation, the matrix of spirit. The color is white.

Beyond *Kether* lies the *Ain Soph Aur*, the "limitless light." It is the primeval beginning of the universe, the unknowable.

THE TREE OF LIFE EXERCISE

There are countless representations of the tree of life—from photos and illustrations to statues and engravings and even jewelry. Choose any of these, and meditate on the nature of the unknowable.

"All that is seen—heaven, earth, and all that fills it—all these things are the external garments of God."

—SHNEUR ZALMAN

THE PICTURES OF MINDFULNESS

Religious images are important mindfulness tools. Statues or pictures of saints, angels, bodhisattvas, and deities can inspire and illuminate us. Incorporate the icons that resonate with you or that represent powers or graces that you would like to invoke for particular circumstances or conditions. For example, you can turn to Ganesh to help you overcome obstacles or to the Virgin Mary to help you practice unconditional love.

A Picture Is Worth a Thousand Petals

Imagery can power the experience of stillness, providing:

- **Centering:** Images focus attention on one idea.
- **Contemplation:** Illustrations may reflect a particular quality that the meditator seeks.
- **Guidance:** Diagrams act as "spiritual maps," depicting the topography of the mind, the soul, or the universe.
- **Integration:** Designs draw attention to the interrelationship of ideas.
- **Inspiration:** Pictures inspire exalted states of mind or feeling.

A VISUAL MEDITATION

Whichever form of imagery you choose for meditation, you can follow a simple fifteen-minute process for allowing it to assist in the goals you are pursuing.

View the image overall for about five minutes, allowing it to "impress" on you. Do not seek detail; see it as a whole. Close your eyes and see the overall image in your mind. If you can't "see" it with your eyes closed, open your eyes and return to the image once more. For the next five minutes, allow your attention to seek the details of the image. A constructive approach is to begin at the base (six o'clock position) and continue in a clockwise direction. You may notice colors, designs, numbers of petals on the flowers, and symbols within the image. Close your eyes and see the details in your mind, repeating the clockwise motion. Continue this process for the second five minutes or until the image is firmly established in your mind. In the last five minutes, sit quietly, waiting for any message that the image might have for you.

CREATE AN ALTAR

An altar is a flat surface decorated with objects and images that support you on your path. Your altar can be made up of objects of encouragement that make you feel supported. Choose items that will remind you of the energy you want to create, the prayers you want to say, the qualities you want to develop in yourself, and the satori you'd like to experience.

There are many ways to make an altar. Keep in mind that the point of the altar is to help you with your mindfulness. With that intention, choose objects that are meaningful and inspirational to you. Here are some ideas for your altar:

- Choose a small table or shelf just for your altar.
- Drape a colored scarf across the surface, a color that speaks to you and whose meaning supports your intentions.

- Place something from outside on the altar, such as seashells from the beach, where you felt peaceful and open, or a small vase of dandelions from your backyard.
- Write out mantras that hold special meaning for you, and place them on the altar.
- If spiritual leaders or symbols inspire you, have those images and/or icons on the altar.
- Place a candle on the altar to remind you of that miraculous natural element that lives outside and inside of you.
- Place notes from loved ones on the altar.

5-Minute Image Exercise

You can tune in to the power of any icon at any time, wherever you are. Keep a statue of St. Christopher in your car for safe travel, sit a Laughing Buddha on your kitchen counter to remind you to lighten up, or make your screen saver a lotus blossom to help you stay on the path of enlightenment.

COLOR ME MINDFUL

The power of imagery depends to a great extent on the impact of its colors. Psychologists, design experts, and healers all agree that the colors around us deeply affect our perceptions. They convey states of mind that are initially perceived visually and gradually filter into our thinking and feeling. A number of approaches to working with color have developed in modern times. Colors have been used in factories to enhance the productivity of workers. Colors are also used to reduce aggression or depression in institutions.

Chromatherapy, or color healing, is used to influence the balance of the body when illness affects functioning and recovery. Many of the current systems are inspired by ancient meditation traditions and the way they use color to harmonize the mind.

CHROMATHERAPY FOR THE SOUL

Colors may be visualized in meditation for healing and maintaining certain states of mind. First, create a "color zone," where you can initially focus on color themes. It should face a blank wall or curtain of a neutral shade so there is no other visual interference. Buy a sturdy easel that can be placed at eye level in your meditation oasis. For this, select colors of matte board that can be cut into medium-size pieces, either 8"× 10" or 9" × 12". Many suppliers have odd cuts for sale, so there is no need to buy a full sheet.

Place the board on the easel in your meditation oasis. It should be to the right or left of your sitting area but not in front of it. You want to be able to move your attention elsewhere if necessary.

Devote at least fifteen minutes to a color session. As with the imagery meditation, give the overall subject a distant gaze for the first five minutes, and then close your eyes. Look at the subject with attention to detail for the next five minutes, and then close your eyes. Gaze at the overall subject again for the last five minutes.

CHOOSING COLORS

Color meditation should be limited to one color per session to allow the color to affect mental and emotional levels.

Red is associated with fire, blood, and vitality. It is the most stimulating of the colors and should be used sparingly in the meditation environment. However, red is also required for clarity of mind when problem solving and raising physical strength after an illness. It stimulates the immune functions and should be followed shortly afterward with a green or blue visualization.

Orange is associated with action, excitement, and warmth. Combining the life force of red with the liveliness of yellow, orange imparts a sense of well-being and regeneration. It is said to influence the body's organs to function optimally and is especially good for digestion. Use orange as a rising agent for emotions and as a mental restorative.

Many cultures see the breath of life in **yellow**. It has a positive effect on the nervous system and stimulates thinking and communication. It is a natural antidepressant, as researchers who study seasonal affective disorder (SAD) have discovered.

Note: This is a different practice from visualization, in which the mind is trained to evoke color and recall it during meditation. The two are not the same practice.

Green is the color of nature, growth, and balance. It is a natural tonic, inviting relaxation. Green calms the body's rhythms. Use it for "grounding" yourself to the present circumstances. Green also assists in emotional poise and balance.

Blue has a cooling effect and counters excited or fearful states of mind. Blue is the color of peace and reflection. Use blue for tranquility, especially after a lot of mental activity. It also instills aspiration and dignity.

Violet combines vitality (red) and serenity (blue). Violet is the color of spirituality. Use it sparingly, however, because it can promote an "otherworldliness" that is not practical. Idealism and intuitive powers are associated with violet.

5-MINUTE COLOR AND BREATH EXERCISE

You can deepen the health benefits of color visualization by adding pranayama breathing exercises. This technique is used therapeutically to remedy chronic health problems.

Start by performing the color visualization exercise. Then begin the color breathing exercise. Take slow, moderately deep breaths. Allow yourself five minutes to do this. As you inhale, visualize the color on the easel lifting off and entering the body, circulating through it. As you exhale, the color fills the space around you and becomes part of the body aura. This may be done to "carry" the color's influence for a time.

INSTANT COLOR EXERCISE

You can instantly imbue your world with the colors of enlightenment. All you need is a can of paint. Paint a wall in your kitchen, your bedroom, your office, your meditation space—wherever a shot of color can lift your spirit.

THE MYSTICAL POWER OF THE TAROT

> *"The true Tarot is symbolism; it speaks no other language and offers no other signs."*
>
> —ARTHUR E. WAITE

The tarot is one of the mystical tools that conveys powerful images for meditation. It is thought to be a codex of the Tree of Life, and many sources show the relationship between the seventy-eight images and the Sephiroth. There is evidence, although obscure, that the system was used for divination in the Middle Ages. Occult legend has it that around 200 B.C.E., the sages of Alexandria, Egypt, recognized the ending of the pagan age. So, they fabricated the system to preserve the wisdom of the ancients in visual form. By placing the system in a deck of playing cards, the sages knew the knowledge could never be lost because the human proclivity for gambling would never cease.

With tarot, you meditate on each image, observing the gestures of the figures, the colors, and the numerical symbolism. You may also use the images to evoke certain states of mind.

Tarot images can awaken the senses and imagination. Every image in the seventy-eight-card deck has symbolic meaning.

The cards in the tarot are divided into two realms: the minor arcana and the major arcana. The minor arcana reflect the arrangement of suits in traditional playing cards: wands (clubs), swords (spades), cups (hearts), and pentacles (diamonds), each with ten numbered and four court cards. These cards convey the images of transitory conditions. The major arcana (sometimes referred to as the "trumps") are distinctive. Numbered from zero to twenty-one (twenty-two in all), they convey images of universal conditions.

Choosing the Right Deck for You

Countless decks are available, many inspired by particular traditions. Some of the most popular include:

- Rider Waite Tarot Deck
- Universal Tarot Deck
- Native American Tarot Deck
- Renaissance Tarot Deck
- Celtic Wisdom Tarot Deck
- Crowley Thoth Tarot Deck
- Aquarian Tarot Deck
- Jungian Tarot Deck
- Mother Peace Tarot Deck

Among other things, each of the major arcana cards represents the path to using the cosmic powers for personal growth. In this sense, they are excellent keys to use in seed meditation. The cards are also believed to subconsciously convey wisdom.

MEDITATING WITH TAROT CARDS

Approach meditation with tarot images in sequence. Begin with 0 (The Fool) and end with 21 (The World). The sequence is important because it represents the progression of cosmic wisdom from the general to the particular spheres of your experience. Even the cards that don't seem pleasing should be included in their natural sequence.

You may begin the sequence with one image for a very short period in one meditation session and go on to the next until you have finished with all twenty-two. Alternately, you may sequentially use one for each day of meditation or even one image for a month of meditation sessions. No matter how much time you allow for each image, you can always return to the beginning and start the sequence again. You can learn a lot each time you use the tarot; for some, it is a continual exercise in symbolic thinking.

UNDERSTANDING THE POWERS IN THE TAROT IMAGES

Each of the tarot images provides information about or "lessons" of personal power. They are conveyed through the colors, figures, and actions depicted in the scenes on each card.

0: The Fool—Fortitude, Enthusiasm. Your insight is awakened into new situations and unfamiliar conditions. In spite of this, your sense of humor and spontaneity come forward, reminding you that you are free to imaginatively use your will.

1: The Magician—Coordination, Synchronization. The order you seek in your life arrives, as well as the skill to translate raw materials into objects of usefulness and beauty. You are in control of your realm, yet still adaptable to new ways of thinking.

2: The High Priestess—Intuition, Retention. You are presented with the scroll of the Akashic record, the cosmic memory of all things past, present, and future. You are able to fuse objectivity with feeling so that you may use this power to make wise decisions and guide others.

3: The Empress—Empathy, Affection. You enter the realm of the Divine Mother, who impels all around her to flourish. She celebrates and shares the fruits of her creative garden with you. You become warm and resourceful, bringing a continual expression of beauty, harmony, and passion in your labors.

4: The Emperor — Organization, Leadership. You become strongly connected to your instincts and keen on assessing people and ideas. You are resistant to harmful influences in thought, health, and your environment.

5: The Hierophant — Cultivation, Enhancement. Like the ancient priest, you draw people together in harmony and peace. You encourage their endeavors and convey wisdom whenever you teach or speak. There are wondrous products of art, architecture, and tradition wherever you are found.

6: The Lovers — Harmony, Loyalty. An angelic spirit overshadows your relationships, blessing the efforts you make with others. You are able to see through the petty concerns of daily life and see the big picture that you are both working toward.

7: The Chariot — Advancement, Initiative. You are able to maintain a forward movement that brings change and adaptation in your life. You are unmoving in your resolve, even though everything around you is in motion. Your resolve also gives you the empathy to understand and guide others forward.

8: Strength — Control, Persistence. The exalted being who restrains the lion is the power you possess to overcome all difficulties. Your commitment to staying on the path you have chosen will be fulfilled in the most auspicious manner.

9: The Hermit — Restraint, Discipline. Circumspection will bring insight into your life so that you may reflect on meanings and truths. Through your endeavors, you will be patient and reminded that everything will take place in its proper time for the best results.

10: The Wheel of Fortune — Adaptability, Versatility. You will approach your challenges with imagination and optimism. Nothing in your life will stay the same; change will allow you to use your talents and receive rewards for your resourcefulness.

11: Justice—Objectivity, Equanimity. There will be balance between your thoughts and actions, and your objectivity will prevail. You will exercise fairness in your dealings, although you must be detached from the confused thoughts and feelings of others.

12: The Hanged Man—Compassion, Idealism. All that has worried you can be seen as transitory and insignificant, compared to your vast inner resources. That which you have placed highest in your life will be achieved in time.

13: Death—Insight, Sensitivity. You will discover that your fears are groundless and that sunrise always follows a dark night. Conditions that appear distressing are transformed into opportunities for valuable experience.

14: Temperance—Moderating, Discriminating. Your angelic presence encourages you to weigh all factors when making choices. You must balance the material and spiritual goals in your life so that you may enjoy progress in both realms.

15: The Devil—Tenacity, Dynamism. Although there is a price to pay for every material possession, your dynamic force can be directed to the work that calls for it. You will make the proper choices in this realm and not be fettered by regret.

16: The Tower—Swift Action, Dedication. Clarity of mind will allow you to maintain calm amidst the storm. Falsehoods will become obvious, and truth will guide you to courageous action for resolving complex problems.

17: The Star—Optimism, Tolerance. Despite setbacks, your hopes will arrive at a favorable destination. Sharing your insights with others, you overcome misunderstandings that have blocked your inner vision.

18: The Moon—Detachment, Impersonality. In a world of confusion, you exercise clarity. This draws others to you who wish to flee from their problems, but you gently guide them toward resolutions.

19: The Sun—Generosity, Humor, Devotion. A return to the carefree world of youth and vitality is possible. By accepting yourself with all your strengths and weaknesses, you are renewed in spirit.

20: Judgment—Dedication, Resolution. No matter what obstacles you face, the inner strength to overcome them is accessible to you. Your goals are meaningful and important.

21: The World—Patience, Endurance. Your life exists in harmonious balance, irrespective of change and appearances. Within this harmony, you realize the illusion of time and understand eternal values.

5-MINUTE MIND–BODY–SPIRIT TAROT SPREAD

Shuffle the cards in the deck while you meditate on the issue, quality, or manifestation you wish to address. Pull three cards and place them right to left. Starting with the left card, turn over each card in turn. The left card represents your mind; the middle, your body; and the third, your spirit. Regard the symbology of the given cards. What is each card telling you? What are they saying together as a spread? Note: If you have trouble reading the cards, consult one of the many books on the subject. *The Tarot Handbook*, by Angeles Arrien, is a good one.

CREATIVE VISUALIZATION: THE IMAGININGS OF YOUR SOUL

A number of approaches to mindfulness use "creative visualization." This method focuses on images that arise from your own imagination, not an external source (images, sounds, sensations). For example, you may begin by visualizing a stream of water slowly coursing down a mountain.

As simple as this suggestion sounds, you may or may not be able to visualize it. This is because some people are more verbal than visual or more apt to hear unrecorded music in the mind than conjure abstract pictures.

IMAGINE THIS MOUNTAIN

Creative visualization takes place with closed eyes. The first step is to immediately place yourself in the picture, before anything else. For example, when you are given the cue to be on a mountain, first, see yourself on the mountain.

Still in the picture, gradually look outside yourself. Look out of your eyes in this scene, seeing your hands and feet, all of your body, the clothing you are wearing. Now look at the vista. See yourself on the mountain, looking down at the view, at the stream as it makes its way down the mountain. Looking up, see the sky. Looking around you, see the brush, trees, and rocks. Maintain your presence on the mountain for as long as possible, at least ten minutes. Coming back to the present, perform the visualization in reverse. Seeing the landscape, look up at the sky; look at the water; and then look down at your clothing, body, hands, and feet. Then open your eyes.

CREATE YOUR OWN VISUALIZATION EXERCISE

Creative visualization is best done on your own, following a script that you may compose and then read or tape for playback in a meditation session. Have fun with it!

It is also important to reverse the visualization after you've gone through it, before you open your eyes and return to ordinary activity. Think of it as taking a journey. You go along a new path, but you want to return to your starting place.

"The soul should always stand ajar, ready to welcome the ecstatic experience."

—EMILY DICKINSON

CHAPTER 11
TUNE IN TO MINDFULNESS

"Any idiot can face a crisis—it's day to day living that wears you out."

—ANTON CHEKHOV

Sooner or later, no matter how hard we have tried to keep our emotions on an even keel as we navigate the inevitable storms of life, something happens that pushes us over the edge—and we feel ourselves start to sink into monkey mind, into hysteria, into that dark night of the soul.

Sometimes it's a major catastrophe that overwhelms us by virtue of its enormity alone. But more often it's a small thing that sets us off—the proverbial straw that breaks the camel's back.

During such doubly stressful times, our usual coping methods fail us. This is when we can call on the strategies that appeal directly to our senses, bypassing the conscious mind altogether, playing upon our subconscious:

- Music to the ears
- Art to the eyes
- Aromatherapy to the nose
- Massage to the skin, including the bottoms of the feet
- Sustenance to the mouth

These are powerful remedies that resonate deep within our bodies, minds, and spirits.

Most are designed to support the ones we have already explored in this book, but adding these elements supercharges their effects.

It's like mindfulness on steroids. So, the next time you feel stressed to the breaking point, you will have at your disposal the most potent aids mindfulness can provide—and you won't even have to think about it. All you'll have to do is breathe.

Sound viscerally impacts our bodies: We can't help moving to the rhythms that we hear. We harness the power of sound to help us live a more mindful life.

Repetitive sounds and words have been used in meditative and mystical practices throughout the ages. They help us maintain spiritual focus by enhancing a particular frame of mind or feeling. Words and sounds are also metaphors for the path to enlightenment. For example, "Abracadabra" is a legendary magical word that is reputed to change lead into gold. It is the same for "Open Sesame," the magical phrase that revealed the cave of the robber chief in *Ali Baba and the Forty Thieves*. Such words are metaphors for opening ourselves to the hidden treasures within us.

THE SOUND OF CREATION

Nearly all traditions cite the creation of the world as an act of sound or exhalation of breath. The Latin *spiritus* and the Greek *pneuma* both indicate breath and spirit. The Hindus envision the god Shiva emoting *spanda*, the cosmic rhythm of the universe, as he dances an eternal dance of life. The ancient Egyptians believed that when the god Thoth spoke the word of creation, all things vibrated into being. In Genesis, creation is brought into being at God's utterance. In all these cosmogonies, the world manifests through sound, or vibration, continuing to expand in the resonance produced by the initial creative utterance.

Modern science is looking at the effect of sound in new ways. Laboratory studies show that music and rhythm can affect cellular life in positive or negative ways, depending on the sounds. In therapeutic settings and learning environments, we are beginning to see how important sound is for clearing the mind.

SOUND OFF EXERCISE

There are as many approaches to using sound as there are meditative styles. You can create your own sound program by listening to what is traditionally used and incorporating what "sounds right" to you. Perhaps you feel drawn to a particular hymn or chant, perhaps an operatic aria or a samba beat interests you, or maybe you feel more at ease with the blues or spirituals.

THE RHYTHM OF THE BRAIN

Sound and rhythm are wired into the human body. Electrical impulses between nerve cells produce all activity in the brain, the control center of the body. These impulses are measured in hertz, or cycles per second. In modern times, researchers have correlated specific states of consciousness with the number of cycles brain waves produce. Brain waves are grouped into four categories: delta, theta, alpha, and beta. However, current research is refining these categories as scientists learn more about the mind, the body, and consciousness.

Delta State: The delta state, which consists of waves of 0.5 to 4.0 cycles per second, is found in deep sleep. This is the lowest cycle observed. In this state, the mind is not attentive to anything in the outside world.

Theta State: The theta state, which consists of waves of 4 to 8 cycles per second, is found in light sleep and deep meditation. This is a "bridge state" between tranquility and drifting off into unconsciousness. Daydreams occur here, as well as events in which the person is conscious but unable to recall details.

Alpha State: The alpha state, in which the waves are 8 to 12 cycles per second, is a relaxed state of nonarousal. Thinking disturbs the alpha state, but attention is active. Reflection and contemplation are associated with this category; it is the target state in most meditation and biofeedback exercises. The normal resting heart rate is about 72 beats per minute. The same rhythm is believed to induce a state of relaxation in the alpha state, and if emulated in music, it can be very hypnotic.

Beta State: The beta state, consisting of waves of 12 to 16 cycles per second, is associated with the engaged mind. Activities such as speaking, relating to others, and learning a new skill fall into the beta state.

Mindfulness moves the mind away from the highly active wavelengths and into the contemplative and reflective wavelengths. Just imagine trying to relax when a road crew is operating a jackhammer outside your window. In the same way, the meditative frame of mind is best reached when the external sounds are conducive to this state and the internal wavelengths in the brain are cooperating. Music and mantra can help facilitate the transition to the deeper, more reflective states.

MANTRA: THE SACRED FORMULA

In many traditions, sound is an integral part of meditative work, and for some, it is sacred language. Sound is a mystical science in yoga and a focusing device in all branches of Buddhism. In these practices, certain tones, spoken or intoned, assist in narrowing attention. In Sufism, Judaism, and Christianity, these tones take the form of recitation of sacred names and phrases to achieve a centered state and oneness with spirit. Chant is also an important part of both religious and secular life in all of the indigenous religions of Africa, Asia, the South Pacific, and the Americas. It unifies the mind of a tribe, while preserving some of the culture's history and beliefs.

Sound and music evoke certain states of mind that reflect mythologic and universal themes. Here are some examples:

- **The Creator:** Sounds that evoke the creative nature, placing the person at the center of the environment. Chants, invocations, and holy names fortify the will and self-awareness.

- **The Peacemaker:** Sounds that promote harmony and tranquility, allowing everyone to meet in agreement. Hymns and ballads are often expressions of peace.
- **The Unifier:** Sounds that join people together in the same spirit of thinking or feeling. Prayers and songs that proclaim divine qualities unify people. Words of inspiration and courage, such as national anthems and military marches, also fall into this category.

In some traditions, mantras are regarded as being as powerful as other meditative activities, such as breathing, posture, and visualization. Just say the word, and you're there!

HOW MANTRAS WORK

In the Middle East, you will hear the call to prayer five times a day. In Europe, the church bells sound daily. At Japanese shrines, wind chimes produce soothing sounds. In these cultures, sounds both awaken the listener and prepare him/her for quieter moments, reminding everyone that peaceful times are approaching.

5-Minute Sound Experiment

Try an experiment to observe how sound affects the environment. Cover the surface of a shallow dish with a small amount of water. Place the dish in front of a stereo speaker, turn on the music, and watch the patterns form on the surface. You'll notice different patterns forming when the musical rhythms and tones change.

When entering into a meditation, we must first empty ourselves of thought. Reciting mantras and toning sounds facilitate this process. Repetitive auditory signals, especially if they are produced in a calming, consistent manner, relax thought. Then, launching into stillness requires less effort. It's important to remember that the science of mantra is a mindfulness tool, but it is not mindfulness. Only when the mind is still is one in a state of mindfulness.

TUNING IN TO YOUR OWN VIBE

Mantras are often linked to vowels that resonate with you in a comfortable, familiar way. Some suggest that the first vowel in your name is the most effective to use in meditation. This is because you are so used to hearing it that it is incorporated in your "vibration."

Many sounds can be used to achieve balance and calm. Toning is one technique that is widely used for meditative and healing work. Toning is really an ancient art form used to restore "harmonic balance" when illness or other crises occur. As with meditations practiced in many traditions, repetitiveness is important. Here's how it works: You repetitively intone specific sounds, giving great care to quality and duration of the intonation. Think of it as mindful humming, though the mouth is not closed in this technique.

VOWEL	LINKED TO
A (aah)	Relaxation, quiet
E (aay)	Humor, acceptance
I (eeh)	Stimulation, attention
O (ooh)	Concentration, focus
U (uuh)	Empathy, harmony

In this system, consonants have highlighting effects, in the same way punctuation gives meaning to the written word. For example, the *Om* mantra combines the focus of the *o* sound with the quality of extension provided by the *m* sound. In this way, words in prayer and meditation have become incorporated in the science of sacred language. While the Hindus resonate to *Om*, Christians and Jews use *amen*, and Muslims use *amin*.

MANTRAS TO USE IN MEDITATION

Sequences of words are also used in meditation to evoke particular states of awareness. Each tradition has its own powerful mantras, although some mantras may be used for specific circumstances. To use them, follow these guidelines:

1. **Confine your use of mantras to one per meditation session.**
2. **Intone the mantra after you are physically settled; this sets the stage for evoking the particular state you are seeking.**
3. **Breathe in, then recite the mantra slowly while exhaling. Intone each vowel for as long as possible, and use the consonants as "punctuation."**
4. **Recite the mantra three times, followed by two to three minutes of silence.**
5. **You may repeat this cycle as many times as you wish, but devote some time, at least ten to fifteen minutes, to conclude in silence and allow the mantra to vibrate within.**

Here are some mantras with pronunciation keys:

- *Yod He Vau He* (yahd-hey-vow-hey): Hebrew for the holy name of God, written as *YHWH* or "Jehovah."
- *Sat Nam* (saaht-namm): In yoga, meaning "I am truth."
- *Om Mani Padme Hum* (ah-um-ma-nee-pad-may-hum): In Buddhism, "Behold, the jewel in the lotus."

THE SOUND OF MEDITATION

In ancient Greek mythology, Orpheus possessed a magic lyre with seven strings, made from an ox skull. Each of the strings was tuned to the motion of the seven planets and could induce the listener to hear the "music of the spheres." It is said that all who heard the sounds of this lyre—animals, planets, people, and even the elements—were transported to divine states of mind.

Throughout time, some instruments have been associated with prayer and meditation. These instruments can be used to expand your practice and experience something new. It's a good idea to experiment with the sounds produced by these tools before you buy them, though. Most stores will not object to your listening for a time to the tones of an instrument you are considering for purchase. Before purchasing, you might also listen to recorded music produced with certain instruments. If they help settle you mentally or emotionally, they will probably be helpful in your meditation oasis as well. Some instruments may be distracting to you. For example, the drum is centering for bodywork but distracting in mental exercises. Meditation instruments should be used to "set the stage" for a meditative session. They can be used to open a sitting that will be followed by silence, or a session can alternate between sound exercises and silent meditation. Here, it is just as important to discern the effects of sound following the experience of it. Instruments to consider include:

- **Drum:** Drums serve to maintain a consistent rhythm and work very well on the physical level, symbolizing the heartbeat. Rattles, shakers, and other percussion instruments work well, too.
- **Bell:** There are so many variations on bell tones that you should choose carefully. Bells are associated with the mental level and symbolize the breath.
- **Chimes:** Chimes are associated with the emotional level and symbolize the sense of touch. The flute and other wind instruments work well, too.
- **Singing Bowls:** Singing bowls are found in unique places, from Tibetan monasteries to South American temples. They may be metal or quartz crystal, and they "sing," or hum, when skimmed with a wood or metal wand. Singing bowls are associated with the inspirational level and symbolize the sense of hearing.

5-MINUTE PLAY RX

Keep your favorite instrument close at hand. Whenever you need a mindfulness break:

- Ring a bell
- Bang a drum
- Shake a rattle

You don't have to be a musician to play any of these classic instruments. Just play, and breathe in the sound of your soul.

MUSICAL CHAKRAS

Music and the chakras have long been combined to balance and invigorate our energy centers. Just as each chakra has a color associated with it, so does each have a sacred sound associated with it. This frequency is known as a *bija*.

To experience a sacred sound meditation, begin in complete silence for about five minutes. You may use a visual of the chakras as they are aligned from bottom to top of the spinal column.

Beginning with the first chakra and progressing upward, intone the *bija*. The sounds and keys for each chakra are as follows:

1. *Lam*, **G**
2. *Vam*, **A**
3. *Ram*, **B**
4. *Yam*, **C**
5. *Ham*, **D**
6. *Om*, **E**
7. **No sound, F**

Intone slowly, first by inhaling and sounding the bija on exhalation. You may intone the bija for each chakra several times to focus on that center. Conclude by intoning the sacred formula, *So Haam* (sew-haaamm), "I am that."

FIRST CHAKRA CRISIS RX

When you find yourself in crisis mode, your fight-or-flight response kicks in, which is a direct challenge to your first chakra, your connection to the earth, the seat of your survival instinct.

When overcome by anxiety, your mind spins in circles of worry. Your heart beats faster, your breath becomes shallow, and your belly becomes upset.

When you are anxious, your energy is predominantly up in your mind. So, you need to bring your energy down. Doing something physical to energize the body will bring energy down from the mind into the body. If the weather permits, get outside to allow the earth's force to help ground you. Whether or not you can get outside, breathe in slowly, feeling your body expand to allow the air to rush inward on the inhale. Envision your connection to the earth as you imagine your inhale going through your body into the ground. On the exhale, chant the first chakra mantra of *lam*. Create a longer exhalation than inhalation to induce relaxation.

Stomp!

Stomping your feet is a great way to ground. If you stomp outside, you leave the energy out there. Let it go. You can even stomp your feet outside each day after work before entering your home. Even if you love your job, this will allow you to keep work stress out of the house.

If you are standing up, imagine your legs as though they have roots growing deeply into the earth. Know you are rooted and connected. If you want to sit down on the ground or floor, then you can imagine the energy coming down from your head out through the first chakra into the earth. For several minutes, breathe and envision energy coming down into the body and flowing into the earth.

LET'S GET PHYSICAL

Adding more physical activity into your day is a preventive means of dealing with anxiety. Literally move your body. This could mean putting on your iPod and dancing for a song (even at your desk) or, while you're sitting down, giving your face, arms, legs, and back a massage. At the very least, you could take a walk down the hall or outside for a five-minute breath of air. Taking a five- or ten-minute break every hour or two during your day will not slow you down; it will help your productivity.

When you're taking a break to move, bring your awareness and attention into your body. If you're walking, feel your legs moving and standing on the ground. Ground that energy. If you're doing a self-massage, notice how your muscles feel. And, don't worry that if you stop the business in your mind for a break, you won't be able to think productively again when you return to your tasks. Leave yourself a note about what you were doing, and when you return, your energy will be able to go back up into your mind and start working again. This is very healthy; it will give your mind a much-needed break and help you practice grounding your energy so, when anxiety arises, you can ground yourself.

ONCE AGAIN, WITH FEELING

Music of every kind—chanting, hymns, Kirtan, jazz, classical, rock and roll, opera, etc.—speaks to us in powerful ways. Whenever things are falling apart, soothe yourself with music. Take your iPod with you everywhere. Turn off the news in traffic and listen to music. Take music (and dance!) breaks during the day at work. Practice yoga to mellow tribal, folk, or indigenous music.

And, when all else fails, sing!

"Music and rhythm find their way into the secret places of the soul."

—PLATO

CHAPTER 12

SET YOUR SIGHTS ON MINDFULNESS

"Art is not a thing, it is a way."

—ELBERT HUBBARD

Beautiful objects—manmade or of the natural world—have long been used around the world as mindfulness tools. From crystals, gemstones, and dried herbs to talismans, amulets, and prayer beads, these age-old objets d'art are beloved in both the East and West for their beauty and power.

But how do they work? How can we use them today? What are you supposed to do with these objects? And, how can we call on their mystical magic to help us when we are in crisis?

SACRED MATERIALS

Many cultures believe that natural objects can awaken special states of mind. The object is believed to "carry" certain powers that nature or human beings place into it. Many materials also have the weight of tradition behind them, and using the "right" materials shows deference or respect for those who have gone before.

In Buddhist cultures, there is a set of powerful gems and metals that you may present at shrines. They are the *Sapta Ratnani* ("previous seven") of gold, silver, lapis lazuli, moonstone or crystal, agate, ruby or pearl, and carnelian. Each represents the purification of your chakras as a gift to the Buddha. Likewise, Native Americans assemble "medicine bags" that contain objects in nature that connect the holder to spiritual forces. They may include rare stones, the bones of animals, and bundles of dried herbs. Let's explore three types of power objects that reflect such purposes: amulets, talismans, and relics.

AMULETS

Amulets are objects worn or carried to protect the individual from negative influences or to bring positive energies. These objects are derived from natural locales, sacred sites, or places where a divine presence has entered the environment. They are usually hard substances, such as bones, glass, metals, gems, stones, shells, and pottery. Amulets may be engraved or enclosed in a metal bezel.

Accoutrements of the Soul

Adorn your altar or meditation space with any number of amulets, talismans, or relics. You can hang them in a special place on the wall or place them by a window to catch the wind and light, where they can serve as constant reminders of the mindfulness you seek.

AMULET CRISIS RX

Whenever you find yourself in a sacred place—anywhere you find peace and inspiration, from churches and temples to the ocean and the mountains—bring home little keepsakes that are small enough to carry on your person either in your pocket or purse or on a bracelet or necklace. Hold this amulet in your hand, or place it on your heart or third eye whenever you need to call on it for extra protection and guidance.

TALISMANS

These objects do not naturally occur, and they may carry an inscription, sigil, or design. Talismans may be made of paper or leather and bear a sacred name, form, or image of a divine force. They may be used to effect special circumstances or events for the wearer or carrier. In

Japan, you can go to a Buddhist shrine and get an *omamori* for a special goal. It's a tiny wooden tablet, placed in a silk bag and worn during meditation. Roman Catholics often wear scapulars to honor saints and to acquire their good qualities and protection through prayer.

RELICS

These objects are the remains of holy persons or places. They may include pieces of clothing, hair, or bone; objects used by the person; or remains of a sacred building. The life force that once embodied relics is believed to still remain in them, providing healing or wisdom to the owner. In Catholic and Orthodox practice, relics are kept in a reliquary at a home or on a church altar. They serve as reminders of the grace that is transferred from the original source to a person through prayer. Mementos from deceased family or friends serve a similar purpose. They remind us of the heritage we wish to preserve.

MEMENTO RX

There are many ways to honor our departed loved ones and invoke their protection and guidance at the same time. Here are some ways to do that:

- Have a ring or bracelet made from your grandmother's silverware
- Keep a favorite book that belonged to your loved one on your desk or by your bed, and open it at random whenever you need comfort or advice
- Frame your grandfather's military medals, and hang them where you can see them
- Wear the religious medal your aunt gave you when you were a child
- Use your father's tools to make a piece of fine furniture
- Use your mother's sewing machine to make a quilt or other item of comfort

GEMS

Gems and semiprecious stones have a mythologic character that is regarded as important to the wearer in many cultures. The belief in birthstones is part of this; it comes from the ancient art of astrology. Birthstones are supposed to transform the inherent weaknesses of each sign in the zodiac and bring out its strengths at the same time. For example, the Cancer native is subject to shifting moods, but the moonstone reflects serenity when it is needed.

Certain moods and states of mind are associated with precious stones. Whether worn or placed in the meditation environment, they are often regarded as important ways to balance and focus the mind and emotions. Gemstones are also associated with the chakras, and wearing them will help balance your chakras.

GEM	MENTAL QUALITY	CHAKRA
Amethyst	Wisdom	Svadhisthana
Diamond	Fortitude	Sahasrara
Emerald	Compassion	Manipura
Ruby	Devotion	Vishuddha
Sapphire	Integrity	Ajna
Selenite	Intuition	Muladhara
Topaz	Knowledge	Anahata

CHAKRA JEWELRY RX

Collect jewelry for each chakra. Wear the appropriate piece whenever you need to invoke the qualities of that chakra. Taking a final exam? Wear topaz. Unsure how to handle a certain problem? Wear amethyst. Finding it hard to deal with a difficult person? Wear emerald.

To the Greeks, the *ametho* (amethyst) is the "preventer of drunkenness." It is believed to protect the wearer against confusion and invites clear thinking. The Chinese believe that jade comes from the bones of dragons. The smooth green variety is believed to possess the five cardinal virtues: charity, modesty, wisdom, justice, and courage. The Native Americans of the southwestern United States believe that turquoise has numerous healing powers, so they fashion it into jewelry to protect the wearer from illness. If the stone cracks, they believe that the residing spirit has departed after absorbing the disease intended for the wearer.

Throughout history, various kinds of stones have been regarded as possessing healing powers. The belief has become transposed in some mind–body practices, such as healing and meditation.

The Rule of Twelve

According to biblical accounts, Aaron, the brother of Moses, was a high priest. Part of his regalia was a breastplate embedded with twelve stones, which symbolized the twelve tribes of Israel. Many also relate this to the twelve astrological signs, but whatever the association, the breastplate supposedly endowed special powers when worn.

In the yogic science of Ayurveda, a repertoire of eighty-four gems is used to assist healing by enhancing certain energies. The ayurvedic physician often recommends either wearing the gems or using them to make "gem waters." The gems are placed in water to rest for a time, and then the patient drinks the water for medicinal purposes. Medieval European physicians used the same procedure.

In meditation, the *navratnas*, or nine healing gems, are used to awaken the body's innate healing powers. The process begins with meditation, followed by visualization of the gem's healing colors and recitation of the planetary mantras that awaken the gem's energies. You then wear the gem to help in the healing process.

NAVRATNA	ENERGY	MANTRA
Cat's eye	Discrimination, self-knowledge	Aum Kaim Ketave Namah Aum
Coral	Determination, purpose	Aum Bhaum Bhaumaye Namah Aum
Diamond	Harmony, creativity	Aum Shum Shu Kraye Namah Aum
Emerald	Self-confidence, problem solving	Aum Bum Budhaye Namah Aum
Lapis lazuli	Preservation	Aum Sham Shanaish Charaya Namah Aum
Pearl	Peace, comfort, intuition	Aum Som Somaye Namah Aum
Ruby	Vitality, resistance, immunity	Aum Hring Hamsah Suryaye Namah Aum
Sapphire	Truthfulness, charity	Aum Brum Brahaspataye Namah Aum
Zircon	Muscular strength	Aum Ram Rahuye Namah Aum

CRYSTALS

In the late-nineteenth century, Jacques and Pierre Curie discovered the phenomenon of piezoelectricity. They found that some crystals, particularly those derived from quartz, rapidly expand and contract on a molecular level when placed in alternating electrical fields. The reverse also occurs when crystals are placed in sound-wave chambers, where they create electrical potentials or voltages. Because of this ability, piezoelectric crystals can be used as either receivers or sources of sound waves in acoustics. The sound waves can run the range of audible to ultrasonic frequencies.

So, metaphysically, crystals—like other materials that come from the depths of the earth—are believed to embody and transmit the subtler frequencies in the environment. This can be beneficial, especially when you place crystals on your altar or in your meditation space. The frequencies from the long-term repetition of mantras or the harmonic atmosphere of serenity, to name just a few, are "stored" in the crystal; and it becomes a sort of organic record of your mindfulness experience. Over time, the crystal may help you relax into mindfulness more quickly whenever you are in your meditation space. Raw rock crystal is reported to be the most effective for this purpose.

Create a Crystal Essence

You can create an "essence" with quartz. Water will copy the crystal's vibration. To create an essence, fill a glass container with crystals, and pour distilled water over them. Note: Some crystals contain potentially poisonous minerals. Be sure to check the chemistry of your crystals before creating an essence. Let sit from several minutes to a couple of hours, and then remove the crystals. You can then place a few drops of the essence in your bath water, or on your pulse points, or in your food or drink. It will last two to three days.

CHAKRAS AND CRYSTAL HEALING

Crystals come from the earth and are believed to have certain healing qualities. When you place the crystals on your body, your intentions help the energy of the crystals enter into your cells. The healing energy vibrates into your physical body and stimulates the chakras.

CLEANSING CRYSTALS

Before using your crystals, it's important to cleanse them of negative energy. You can cleanse them by leaving them out overnight in the light of a full moon. The energy of the moon is said to clear them, returning them to their own pure vibration. There are other ways to cleanse crystals of negative energy:

- Go to a fresh spring, and bathe your crystal, with the points facing downward.
- Create a salt solution using sea salt and water. Use only sea salt and cool water. Place the crystal in the solution, point down, and leave it to cleanse overnight.

- Bury your crystal in a jar of dry sea salt or dried herbs or outside in the earth overnight.
- "Smudge" your crystals by burning sage leaves and clearing the air around the crystals with the smoke from the burning sage. You can buy sage already bundled specifically for smudging, and one bundle can be used several times.

Use glass or ceramic containers to cleanse your crystals. And, before cleansing crystals in water, make sure your crystals aren't water soluble, or else they will dissolve. As you cleanse your crystals, imagine white light flooding through them. Send them love from your heart, and fill them with an intention, such as "I intend for this crystal to cultivate easeful healing for my highest good." It's always best to use the word "ease" or "easefully" when you set intentions for healing.

CHOOSING CRYSTALS FOR EACH CHAKRA

Books and charts differ about which crystals will help heal each chakra. You can cultivate your own relationship to crystals and find which ones you can connect with. There are some standards with each chakra that follow the rainbow as a guide: red for Muladhara, orange for Svadhistana, yellow for Manipura, green or pink for Anahata, blue for Vishuddha, indigo for Ajna, and a white/clear or amethyst crystal for Sahasrara.

Allow yourself to be creative with the crystals. Find out what particular crystals are known for, and match them up to what you might need at each chakra. Because each person is different, no one prescription will suit everyone. As a starting point, though, the rainbow guide will work well.

The colors of the rainbow associated with each chakra will help bolster a deficient chakra. If you have an excessive chakra, rather than using a crystal to enhance that chakra, try using a crystal at the chakras below or above the excessive one to help diffuse the excess energy.

Once you have cleansed your crystals, keep them in a nice pouch on your altar or in another special place. If you keep them in a place where you can see them, then every time you see them, you can be reminded of the natural beauty and healing energy that comes from the earth.

Set Your Intention Crystal Healing Exercise
Crystal healing potential is activated by the mind's intention. Just like everything else on earth, crystals vibrate at certain frequencies. When you place the crystal near the chakra you want to balance, the crystal increases the healing vibration of your intention. Crystals amplify the energy you send through them and draw out negative energies from the body.

PLACEMENT OF CRYSTALS
One of the ways to use crystals for healing is to place one in your nondominant hand. Meditate on the crystal, its healing power, and the intention you want to infuse it with. Hold the crystal in your hand, and then move your hand toward the area of your body needing healing. Hold it there, with the crystal against your body, and meditate on its healing energy. On each exhale, envision the crystal drawing negative energy out. On each inhale, imagine the body absorbing the crystal's healing energy.

If you want to do this lying down, you can lay the crystals on your body and meditate with them there while you lie down. Some say that the less you touch the crystals, the better because their energy will remain purely their own. Others say, as long as you keep your energy positive and focused on your healing, then your own hands and energy will enhance the crystal's effects.

After you've finished using the crystals for this visualization, take some time for the healing effects to integrate. Give yourself a few moments, at least, before resuming other activities. Allow the effects to sink in.

You could also use crystal healing after another chakra healing practice. For example, you could start your chakra healing session with a yoga sequence and then follow it up with crystal healing. Or, while you do your yoga sequence, you could take a few sips of your crystal essence.

Remember: An essence, or elixir, has the vibrational quality of the crystal used to infuse it. To preserve your essence for more than a couple of days, place it in a dark glass bottle, and add the same amount of vodka as liquid as a preservative. Keep the bottle out of sunlight and out of contact with other bottles.

CRYSTALS MATCHED WITH CHAKRAS

There are many kinds of crystals to choose from. Here are some examples of crystals you can use at each chakra when following the rainbow as your guide.

CHAKRA	CRYSTAL
Root	bloodstone
Sacral	carnelian
Solar plexus	citrine
Heart	rose quartz or jade
Throat	lapis lazuli or turquoise
Third Eye	amethyst
Crown	clear quartz or moonstone

With these suggestions as your guide, you will find crystals of different shapes and sizes. It doesn't matter which one you choose. Choose what you feel attracted to, and remember to cleanse it before each use.

BEADS

Just about every culture has a custom of using beads in meditation or prayer. They help the user to focus on recitation and counting. Ceremonial beads include:

- **Rosary:** Used for Catholic prayer, the rosary consists of five sets of beads, each consisting of ten small beads and one larger. These sets are joined in a loop by a crucifix. An Anglican version uses four sets of seven "week" beads, with four "cruciform" beads marking the four directions.

- **Muslim Prayer Beads:** These prayer beads are used to silently recite the ninety-nine names of God. The ninety-nine beads are joined in a loop by a tassel.

- **Mala:** In Hindu and Buddhist meditation, 108 beads are strung together. Some malas are fabricated from sandalwood, which can be infused with scented oils. In the yogic tradition, rudraksha ("Rudra's tears") and tulasi ("holy basil") beads are used.

- **Chinese Meditation Balls:** The two metal balls fit into the palm of the hand and musically resonate when moved around by the fingers.

- **Prayer Stones:** The cool feeling of these rounded stones, also called touchstones, can be relaxing. You can carry them in your pocket or your purse to the office desk or dentist's chair as psychic reinforcement for calm.

"Listen to your life . . . Touch, taste, smell your way to the holy and hidden heart of it because in the last analyses all moments are sacred moments and life itself is grace."

— FREDERIC BUECHNER

CHAPTER 13
BREATHE IN MINDFULNESS

"Nothing is more memorable than a smell. One scent can be unexpected, momentary and fleeting, yet conjure up a childhood summer beside a lake in the mountains."

—DIANE ACKERMAN

The sense of smell is one of the most powerful instruments we possess to connect the outer world with inner states. Scent is inhaled through the nose, traveling through the olfactory nerves into receptors in the brain. From there, scent creates changes in the limbic system, a primitive area in the brain that governs emotions and memory. It is through this simple act of inhaling that molecules of scent can impact our psychological state.

In the 1970s, Robert Tisserand, a researcher in the science of smell, produced a body of work inspired by the studies of Dr. Jean Valnet, in France. Tisserand demonstrated the tremendous influence and potential of aromatic plants for the health of body and mind. He was one of the first to write an exposition on the science of aromatherapy, which now has become a buzzword in everyday business and leisure. Tisserand made the connection between aromatic substances and the human endocrine system. In addition, he observed studies showing that scent could actually alter brain-wave activity.

Marketers have long since known about the power of smell to seduce customers, and the field of aromatherapy is rapidly developing scent for healing. A Japanese website has started mapping unusual scents around the world so that aficionados can sample them. In 2009, at Brigham Young University, researchers found that smells associated with cleanliness (in this case, citrus-scented Windex) led test subjects to reciprocate trust. Take some of this wisdom into your practice space: Keep it clean and lightly scented with something calming and inspiring.

MAP YOUR MOOD WITH SCENT

Scent is big business. Scientists who specialize in understanding the effects of scent on mood and mind are called odorologists. In recent years, odorologists have been investigating which smells influence states of mind in order to create a "mood map" that reveals the secrets of scent. Preliminary results show that citrus is mentally stimulating, vanilla is relaxing, and rose is calming. For therapeutic use, odorologists have confirmed that cucumber helps claustrophobics.

And, that's not all. The presence of certain smells can influence performance. Experiments have shown that children test better in school with floral scents in the atmosphere, while adults exercise harder (without noticing it) when strawberry is released into the environment.

THE SMELL DIET

One of the more interesting developments is research in Japan on weight loss using scent. Researchers at Shiseido, a well-respected cosmetics giant, are releasing a body lotion that they claim will stimulate the brain to discharge hormones that burn fat. Some of the ingredients they have disclosed are grapefruit and pepper. Other studies show the scents of apple and banana have a similar effect on test subjects who are dieting.

Department stores have caught on to this phenomenon and use it extensively. To stimulate customer interest and patronage, stores are releasing scents through potpourri "cookers," ventilation systems, and old-fashioned spray bottles.

It's important to be aware of these trends. Scent has always been known to have a subliminal effect, and in recent times, science has confirmed this knowledge. As a result, fragrance is used even more to influence our thinking and moods. A positive way to counter the trend is to use scent in meditation, when our senses are functioning optimally. By wisely choosing fragrances that support the meditative environment and our own goals, we may become the cartographers of our own mood maps.

The Pheromone Connection

The ability of a scent to attract the attention and interest of a subject is based on its concentration of pheromones (from the Greek, "to transfer excitement"). Pheromones are complex molecular structures that transmit signals through the air via scent. Animals and insects have them and so do humans. Pheromones play a considerable role in creating the magnetic attraction between people.

MINDFULNESS AND ESSENTIAL OILS

Essential oils are mindfulness tools that can enhance mental clarity and relaxation. Certain scents protect, purify, elevate feeling, and repel negative thoughts, especially when applied to certain parts of the body:

- **Brow:** The intuitive sense
- **Crown:** The mental processes
- **Feet:** Purification for healing, trauma
- **Hands:** To bring grace to one's work following meditation
- **Heart:** The emotional plane
- **Solar plexus:** The physical functions

A CATALOG OF SCENT

To be most effective, essential oils should be pure and uncut. Oils should never be kept in plastic containers. Traditionally, essential oils are stored in amber or blue glass to protect them from ultraviolet light. They should be touched on the body with cotton or an eyedropper since placing the fingers directly on the bottle opening can alter the purity of the scent within. Essential oils need to be diluted in a base carrier before being applied to the skin.

OIL	USE
Cedar	Dispels sluggishness, lethargy
Cinnamon	Treats fatigue, depression
Eucalyptus	Has a cooling influence; helps with anger
Frankincense	Maintains meditation focus; inspirational and rejuvenating
Geranium	Has an uplifting vibration; addresses anxiety
Jasmine	"Softens" the emotions; treats listlessness, fear
Lavender	Aids memory and alleviates mental stress; old-fashioned headache remedy
Neroli (orange blossom)	Counters insomnia, nervous tension
Patchouli	Clarifies problems; encourages objectivity
Pine	Lessens claustrophobia; elevates emotions
Rose	Functions as an antidepressant; effective for grief
Sage	Supports healing processes, the purification of space
Sandalwood	Evokes confidence and supports meditation overall; revered in Ayurveda

AROMATHERAPY MASSAGE

A trained professional gives aromatherapy massage by selecting the appropriate oils to mix in a base carrier oil. The essential oils are highly potent and so are not meant to be applied directly to the skin. A base carrier oil is a pure oil, such as extra-virgin cold-pressed olive oil or sesame oil, that can be used to dilute essential oils.

If you do get expert advice and would like to do self-massage with essential oils, get the best carrier oil that you can, from a specialist store. What you put on your body gets absorbed into your body, so you want only the purest and best oil when you apply it to your skin.

Then, add drops of the essential oil to the base carrier. A typical recipe is to measure the amount of base oil in milliliters and then divide that number in half to give you the maximum number of drops of essential oil that you will need.

Note: Test the mixture of essential oils and base carrier on the skin of the receiver, first, by applying a small amount to the inside of the wrist, behind the knee, and/or in the crease of the elbow. Check the spot twenty-four hours later to see if the skin had a reaction or not.

5-Minute Aromatherapy Self-Massage

After testing the oil on the skin to make sure there is no allergic reaction, you can do a healing self-massage. First, put a couple of drops of the mixture of base oil and essential oil onto your hands, and rub your hands together to stimulate the scent of the oil. Bring the palms of your hands up to your face, and inhale the scent for several breaths. Then, gently begin to massage the top of your head, at the crown. Next, slowly progress down the body, giving your body the attention it deserves. Continue to inhale the aroma that gently wafts through the air.

When you've finished with the massage, relax. Allow the effects of the massage to sink in. Envision the healing occurring. Enjoy the process!

DIFFUSING ESSENTIAL OILS

Instead of applying a mixture of base carrier oil and essential oils to the skin, you can receive the healing benefits of essential oils by diffusing them. Specific diffusers are made to use with essential oils. Read the directions; each diffuser works differently. The point of the diffuser is to release the aroma and the healing properties of the essential oil into the air. This has a humidifying benefit to combat the dryness in the air, and it helps sanitize and infuse the air with healing properties. For example, you can diffuse lavender into the air to promote relaxation and serenity or tea tree oil for its antiviral and antibacterial properties.

5-Minute Energetic Self-Massage

You can do an aromatherapy energetic self-massage without touching your body. For the energetic massage, mix the essential oils with a high-quality base carrier oil. Place a few drops of the elixir into your hands. Rub your hands together to release the scent of the oils. Bring the palms of your hands to your face to inhale the scent for several breaths, and call to mind the healing properties of the oils. Inhale and exhale several times. Then, hold your hands about six to ten inches from your body, and do an energetic sweep of your entire body. Slowly, sweep downward, brushing away unwanted disturbance in the energy field. After you've completed this, relax for several moments. Notice the effects. Then, wash your hands with cold water.

STEAMING WITH ESSENTIAL OILS

Especially at times of the year when the air is dry or in dry climates, steaming with an essential oil is a wonderful way to receive therapeutic benefits.

1. Have a towel and your essential oil nearby.
2. Use a bowl that is approximately 10 to 12 inches in diameter.
3. Boil enough water to fill the bowl ½ to ⅔ full.
4. Pour the steaming water into the bowl, and then add one drop of the essential oil to the bowl.
5. Lean your head into the flow of the steam, and put the towel over your head to cover your head and the bowl.
6. Inhale deeply through both nostrils; exhale gently through the mouth. Repeat this several times.

7. If you would like to, close one nostril with your finger, and inhale and exhale through one nostril at a time to make sure that each side is receiving the benefits.
8. If one drop of the essential oil wasn't strong enough or if the scent diminishes, add another drop. It's doubtful you will need more than two drops of the essential oil.
9. When you are finished steaming, sit down. Take a moment to notice the effects. Practice this two to three times per day if you're working with a particular imbalance or the onset of a cold.

Steaming with an essential oil is a quick way to get the benefits of the essential oils. Infused with healing properties, the vapor rises into the nasal passages, immediately entering your system. Steaming is an effective, easy, and soothing way to feel the benefits of essential oils.

TAKE A SOULFUL BATH

Another way to enjoy steaming with an essential oil is to use the elixir in a warm bath. First, dilute the essential oil in a base carrier oil. Then, pour about a fourth of a cup of the mixture into your bathtub. The oil will absorb into your body through your skin, and as you inhale, you will bring the oil's healing qualities into your body through your nostrils. This is a soothing, relaxing, and natural way to feeling well.

THE SWEET SMELL OF ENLIGHTENMENT

In the Middle East, perfume is regarded as the "soul" of the plant. For the French, scent is the music of the senses. When mosques were built in the Middle Ages, the mortar was mixed with rose oil so the walls would exude a divine odor at midday. In a similar way, we can use scent to evoke moods that support meditation. While doing this, the innate healing qualities of certain scents can also assist in physical and emotional well-being.

In your sacred space, you may use items that provide a continuous scented atmosphere. There are hot and cold diffusers, which require an electrical outlet to operate. Scented oils or waters are placed in a receptacle that releases the mist in timed or graduated amounts. Choose one that will shut off automatically when emptied. You can also moderate the scented atmosphere on your own by using spray bottles whenever you choose. In that way, you can alternate different scents as a "sense exercise." Just be sure to point spray bottles away from the walls and furniture when you use them.

Note: Incense burners and potpourri bowls heated with candles should be used with caution. For incense burners, choose terracotta, clay, stone, or metal holders that have ample room to catch the ashes. Incense wands last a little more than half an hour, which is also a good way to time a meditation session.

THE POWER OF INCENSE

Incorporating incense into your meditation brings the "soul" of contemplation into the atmosphere. Entering a room where incense has been burning can instantly relax you. Even the residue of incense is calming, as it penetrates furniture, curtains, and even pet fur.

BURNED OFFERINGS

In ancient Mexico, the Maya manufactured and traded incense in great quantities. Copal incense, taken from a variety of Central American pine trees, was believed to purify the dwelling. It was also pressed into cakes decorated with the heads of their deities and carried through crop fields to sanctify them.

Native North Americans also purify spaces with dried herbs. Small bundles of cedar, tobacco, sweetgrass, and sage are burned and used to smudge windows and doors to prevent harmful influences from entering a sacred space.

Incense imparts a feeling of the sacred and can support the atmosphere of meditation. Here are some suggestions for incense selections:

- **For facilitating breath work during pranayama:** Eucalyptus, pine, and lavender are clean and penetrating scents.
- **For mental focus:** Basil, geranium, and frankincense penetrate deeply through the emotional sphere and have lasting power.
- **For purifying emotions:** Jasmine, vetiver, sage, and cypress have a calming effect on mood.
- **For neutralizing stress:** Rosemary reduces melancholy, and scents of the mint family (peppermint, spearmint) are mentally uplifting.
- **For an inspirational atmosphere:** Patchouli, sandalwood, and myrrh are the traditional ingredients for liturgical incense.

THE MERITS OF INCENSE

In Japan, KŌ (incense) is regarded as a sacred substance. During the Edo period, the art of *Kodo*, the "Way of Incense," arose. An event similar to the tea ceremony is arranged, in which fragrant substances are burned for reflection. The Ten Virtues of Burning KŌ are as follows:

- Incense opens the mind to divinity.
- Incense cleanses the mind.
- Incense divests the mind of worldly impurities.
- Incense awakens the mind.
- Incense encourages the mind in solitude.
- Incense affords the mind leisure when it is busy.
- One cannot burn too much incense.
- Even a little incense is not enough.
- Age does not affect the efficacy of incense.
- Habitual use of incense causes no harm.

GROWING YOUR MINDFULNESS GARDEN

Plants are more than stems, roots, and seeds. Laboratory experiments conducted over the past three decades suggest that plants have some form of consciousness and react to sound—from music to the human voice.

We all know someone who has a "green thumb." He/She seems to be able to grow anything effortlessly and his/her home is filled with delightful plants and flowers. What may distinguish these people from the rest of us who labor over scrawny little vines is the ability to become meditative with the plant. How is this done? Most gardeners will agree that, when you become involved with the growing, feeding, and caring of a plant, you establish a subtle relationship with it. And, in that relationship, there isn't much room for your own thoughts and feelings. There is only the soil, water, and the seed.

Working with nature in this way is an exercise that removes you from the constraints of time. The rhythm of planting, nurturing, and watching the plant grow and yield its benefits is timeless because it's always going on around us. Becoming part of that rhythm is rather effortless, too. It's really just a matter of finding your plant soul.

FIND YOUR PLANT SOUL

Just as there are as many meditation styles as there are people, so there are plants for everyone who wants to experience this relationship with nature. You can find the type of plant that resonates to your personality and subtly imparts its qualities to you and your meditation environment.

To learn something about the care of plants and flowers, look at horticulture catalogs. At the same time, study the photographs of the mature plants, and make note of the colors and types that appeal to you. Consider some basics of what you want from the plant. Will it be culinary (to eventually eat), functional (to provide oxygenation or ward off insects), or decorative? Balance the basics with the subtle qualities the plant can provide: scent, color, a feeling of calm, healing, and beauty.

Start out with just a few growing things in your sacred space. If they become prolific, all your meditation time may wind up being devoted to their care.

5-Minute Plant Food for the Soul

You can evoke the essence of your plant soul simply by filling a vase with flowers and placing it on your altar or desk or in your sacred space or any room in the house. Notice how just the presence of a living thing or the sweet scent of freshly cut blooms can change the energy of the space—and yours along with it.

Experience the plants and flowers directly. Visit nurseries, flower shows, and public gardens. Ask the caretakers about plant qualities they have learned from experience. If a particular plant appeals to you, spend some time looking at it and reflecting on its qualities. Be attentive; you may get a response.

"Trees are happy for no reason."

—OSHO

5 MINUTES TO A MINDFUL LIFE

Together we have explored the many ways in which we can quiet our minds, listen to our bodies, reconnect with our spirits, and commune with the divine—all of which helps us to live a more mindful life . . . minute by minute, hour by hour, day by day.

Take these strategies with you, and incorporate them into your daily life. Let go of your worries, your fears, and your misperceptions—and breathe in love, compassion, and joy.

You'll think better, you'll feel better, and you'll live better.

All it takes is five minutes.

Oh soul,
You worry too much.
You have seen your own strength.
You have seen your own beauty.
You have seen your golden wings.
Of anything less,
Why do you worry?
You are in truth
The soul, of the soul, of the soul.

—Rumi

INDEX